BETTER DEAD THAN DIVORCED

THE TRIALS OF PANAYOTA: A TRUE STORY

LUKAS KONANDREAS M.D.

A
TRUE STORY
BASED ON

_My memories as an 8-year-old
personally involved in this story,
_More than 160 interviews with those close to the events,
_Newspaper Accounts of the events,
_Court Records.

PART I

CHAPTER 1:
THE VIRGINITY TEST

FROM THE MOMENT, SHE BLOSSOMED into a beautiful young woman trouble seemed to follow Panayota wherever she went. And that trouble, I'm sure her cousin Thanasis would have insisted, had a name: George Nitsos. Charming, gregarious, slippery—George Nitsos had no regard for the conservative mores of his community. He was the kind of young man who inspired fathers to keep their daughters under lock and key, the kind of young man whose smile said one thing while his eyes said another. After he took an interest in my aunt, it wasn't long before she found herself the subject of village gossip.

Thanasis was serving as Panayota's chaperone the night she was forced to reveal a terrible secret to her family.

"Are you ready?" he asked after helping her dismount from his horse.

At the moment, his gaze rested on his frightened cousin, who he knew was about to receive a severe tongue-lashing from the rest of the family. Though he didn't approve of Panayota's errant ways, Thanasis nevertheless felt sympathy for her plight. The two had just returned from the nearby bigger village, where she had met with a doctor at his office for her second virginity test. The first test, conducted weeks earlier under nebulous conditions, had yielded unclear results and had earned the headstrong young girl a stern reprimand from her family. This

1

time, however, the findings were incontrovertible: she was no virgin.

"Yes," Panayota said nervously.

Thanasis nodded stoically and turned to secure his horse outside her family's two-story stone residence. Panayota disappeared inside to face her family.

Thanasis, hoping to spare Panayota the prying eyes and wagging tongues of her fellow villagers, had waited for darkness to fall before escorting her home from the doctor's office. During the ride, Panayota had admitted she'd indeed had sex with George. She liked him. He had pledged to marry her. There was only one solution, thought Thanasis, still trying to shake off the embarrassment he'd felt at the doctor's office: George would have to make good on his promise.

Unfortunately, nothing could be done to protect Panayota from her family's scorn. By the time Thanasis had followed his cousin inside, every adult member of her family—her mother, siblings, aunts, uncles, cousins, grandparents—was looking at her expectantly. Had she failed the test?

Panayota, staring at her feet, spoke in a hushed tone. "The doctor said I'm not a virgin."

Thanasis found the tension in the home nearly unbearable. Would they chop her into pieces and throw her into the brook, as one of her elders had warned her only a few short weeks ago? He suspected such talk was exaggerated, but he also knew the emotions that fueled it were combustible.

Who would speak first? Skevi, Panayota's widowed mother? One of her uncles or aunts? A grandparent? A cousin? What kind of invective would they spit at the fearless young girl?

James, Panayota's younger brother, was the first to react, but not with words. He leapt at his sister, shoving her violently toward the fireplace.

Panayota lost her balance and fell backward into the burning embers.

While Thanasis and the other men rushed forward to restrain James, a screaming Panayota pulled herself from the fireplace with the help of the women, who were now furiously beating the flames from the girl's clothing. Singed but not seriously injured, she turned and fled outside as soon as the flames had been tamped out, leaving behind the stench of burnt fabric.

Skevi, still screaming in horror, could barely be heard above the men-folk, most of whom continued to unleash a blue streak of vitriol even after Panayota's tearful exit.

"I'm going to kill Linatsas!" thundered James, whose curses were now aimed equally at his sister and his best friend.

Known by many in the village as "Linatsas," George Nitsos had earned the nickname after purportedly being caught red-handed stealing a lamb, which, according to village legend, he had tried to smuggle away in a burlap bag, or linatsa. Although he would deny the story to his dying day, it would nevertheless haunt him throughout his life.

"Why did I let the bastard into my house?" James growled.

One of eight children, George hailed from Kupaki, although his father was often absent, having traveled to America to find work. For a short stretch in the 1920s, the Nitsos family had returned to Greece but on their next trip back to America, George was left behind and returned with a few of his siblings to Kupaki.

"Why did his father leave him behind?" James lamented. "Couldn't he have taken him to America?"

George's homecoming had reunited him with James, his old classmate and good friend. Not long afterward, George had met James's fetching older sister, and Panayota had been courting trouble ever since.

"I'm going to kill him," James repeated, only with less conviction now and in a much softer voice. As he spoke, he stared out the window to the west in the direction of George's house, which was only 150 yards away. He was beginning to calm down.

It helped that the women were urging him to keep quiet, lest he be heard by neighbors and add insult to humiliation.

Thanasis and the other men in the room released James from their collective grip, and soon the room fell silent.

3

Aggelo, Thanasis's sister, was the first to speak up. She leveled an accusatory stare at James. "Do you know what you have done?"

"I don't care," he muttered angrily. "Let her go to hell forever."

"James, can you hear what you're saying? What will you do if your sister throws herself down the ravine?"

James flinched visibly. Was he finally coming to his senses?

As Thanasis studied the young man's round, innocent face for clues, he tried to put himself in James's shoes. How would he feel if his best friend had shamed his sister? Would he feel duped? Betrayed? He would certainly be brimming with anger. It was obvious that George had viewed his friendship with James as a way to his sister's heart. Though they were the same age, James clearly looked up to George. His wide-eyed admiration served as silent applause to George, for whom life was a performance. George had always struck Thanasis as the kind of performer whose self-esteem sky-rocketed or nosedived according to his audience's response. In James, he could count on rapt admiration.

George was the friendly extrovert who knew all about life in the big city, the sophisticate who could tell a seemingly serious story with a straight face until delivering the punch line, which never failed to double over his listeners with laughter. He didn't boast of his family in America. Instead, he poked fun at their respectability in a good-natured way. He was generous with his friends, often sharing the American dollars that his father mailed to him. For many shy young men, to pal around with George Nitsos was to bask in reflected glory; it was an easy way to earn the attention of the opposite sex without committing to the hard work of courtship or risking the rejection that came with it. The village girls, meanwhile, couldn't resist his boyish charm. He was effusive with his praise, often lavishing it on the fairer sex with such hyperbole that it bordered on the ludicrous. The conservative community of Kupaki, on the other hand, frowned when young girls accepted the overtures of this rogue with nothing more than a smile and a blush.

"Oh, my girl, my girl," Skevi lamented.

"I'll go and look for her myself," Aggelo said. "All of you just try to keep quiet. And don't start another round of weeping and swearing. You'll have the whole village talking about this for months."

"Do you need a flashlight, Aggelo?" James asked.

Thanasis's sister, still clearly peeved, rolled her eyes. "You think of everything, don't you, James?" she said in a sweet voice laced with acerbic undertones. "Now that you've taken care of all the other things, maybe I should just run this little errand of finding your sister before she kills herself."

With that, Aggelo stepped out into the darkness.

Before beginning her search for Panayota, Aggelo made a mental checklist of all the locations where the desperate girl might go to hide. Every village had places where people could go when they wanted to be alone, and Kupaki was no different. She would start with the village spring, which vibrated with gossip and energy during the waking hours but was a solemn, peaceful haven at night. It was near Panayota's home, near as well as where she worked, and offered several hiding places beneath the canopy of trees.

First, she needed to catch her breath. She leaned back against the trunk of an ancient maple tree and waited for her breathing to slow down and her eyes to adjust to the darkness, the spring gurgling just a few feet away.

Skevi's lament—"Oh, my girl, my girl"—echoed in Aggelo's mind. Not so long ago, Panayota had been an innocent young girl, someone who worked hard at school and at home. Always well groomed and neatly dressed, she was known for her sense of humor. People talked about Panayota as *tsahpina*, a nearly untranslatable Greek word that encompassed graciousness, efficiency, and elegance. Now she was hiding in the dark, a blot on her family's honor.

Aggelo listened quietly for an exhale or a sob that would lead her to her cousin. Soon she heard footsteps coming toward her. They were too heavy to belong to Panayota, who was small, slim, and light-footed. This was the heavy tread of a man. Her heart skipped a beat at the thought of being caught outside without a male chaperone. What madness had inspired this adventure? Why hadn't she asked her brother Thanasis or one of the other men to set off in search of Panayota?

The answer, she knew, was a simple one: her cousin would be more likely to trust her.

When the man closed to within a few feet, Aggelo breathed a sigh of relief. It was James.

"Hey!" she whispered.

Her cousin let out a terrified cry, clutching his chest. Then, after taking a few seconds to calm himself, he joined Aggelo against the same stout maple trunk. As he did, he launched into a five-minute tirade that made use of every curse in the Greek language.

Aggelo waited for him to finish. "Don't you think you've done enough?" she scolded him. "You're the last person Panayota will want to talk to if she's somewhere out here. Do us all a favor and go home."

To Aggelo's relief, James did just that. As soon as he was safely on his way, she took a few tentative steps, just enough to escape the noise from the gurgling spring. Then she whistled softly, imitating the call of a nightingale, and waited.

Panayota. Age about 18.   *Panayota. Age about 23.*

CHAPTER 2:
TIRED OF SECRETS

PANAYOTA HAD FOUND A HIDING place in her uncle's terraced garden, just below the springs, where she sat on a rock and leaned against one of the stone walls, waiting silently. Stars lit up the night sky. Fireflies hovered and danced in the cool night air. On distant hilltops, shepherds stoked fires to stay warm and keep the jackals at bay. Nearly every home in the village had a vegetable patch, not to mention stairs and balconies decorated with potted flowers, vegetables, and basil—all of which filled the air with a heady fragrance. The ripening fruit from trees, too, could be detected in the cool breeze. But nothing compared to the pungent aroma of honeysuckle, which was particularly powerful at night and filled Panayota's nostrils with its sweet scent.

She was still shocked by the savagery of her brother's response, still numb from the indignity of being forced to endure not one but two virginity tests. Was it a crime to love George Nitsos? Part of her wanted to answer Aggelo's soft whistle, but part of her wanted only to run away with her lover, to disappear forever. Then again, sometimes she wished she'd never met George Nitsos. Before he had come along, life had been so much simpler.

She met George not long after going to work for her neighbors, who had offered to take care of her in return for her help with household chores and work in the fields. Her mother, after mulling over the idea, had consented. Life had been hard since her father's passing, and Skevi had no doubt thought she was giving Panayota, just thirteen at the time, an opportunity at a better life. And she had been right. Panayota had fit in right away with her neighbors, who never mistreated her.

Then one day Panayota met her brother's friend, George. Handsome, lean, charismatic, George was a consummate flirt and often said things that made the young girl's face blush and her heart race. The two began seeing each other secretly, meeting in the vineyards near the village spring, which was perfectly situated between her boss's house and her home. As the tone and content of their conversations grew more intimate, Panayota suddenly realized one day that she was being courted— and that she was enjoying these clandestine rendezvous.

When word of their affair reached her mother, brother, and her cousins, the Konandreases, Panayota earned an earful. She was called a slut and told she had dishonored her family. When she revealed the truth, which was that she had done nothing to compromise her innocence, she was met with distrust and contempt. James had recommended she be seen by a doctor, who would be able to prove or disprove her claims of innocence. The virginity test, however, had yielded murky results, which the doctor had blamed on poor lighting and a lack of necessary equipment.

Panayota, still leaning against the stone wall in the darkness, flinched involuntarily. The memory of her first virginity test still sent her flesh crawling. She had been so terrified during the test that the doctor had admonished her for her lack of proper cooperation, which he had said had marred the results. Not that anything had changed after the test. George, after staying away for a while to avoid further inflaming Panayota's family as well her boss's family, returned at the time of the wheat harvest. During the noonday siesta, he could be heard crooning a love song to Panayota:

Vipers hissing venomous wrath
Keep my love and me apart.
But I'll cross their spiteful path
To be with you, my sweetheart.

Panayota didn't think her family or her boss were snakes, of course. They were merely trying to protect her honor, along with their own reputations as upstanding members of the community. Her boss, intent on avoiding further scandal, had put in place several restrictions to curb Panayota's behavior and had begun watching her closely. Just like her family, they felt impugned by George's indecent behavior.

Panayota nevertheless admired her suitor's temerity. She began meeting him again, only now under the cover of darkness, furtively seeking his embraces in the vineyards and vegetable gardens in the neighborhood. After her boss caught Panayota sneaking out one night for another rendezvous, the same drama played out once more: admonishment, followed by denial, followed by a virginity test.

This time, though, the doctor's findings had left no room for doubt. She had dishonored her family.

Panayota, shivering in the cool night air, wrapped herself in her arms. She knew that she had no power to change things. She was a woman. George was a man. They lived by two different codes. While he could prowl the neighborhood with impunity, she could only be seen in public with a male chaperone. Even in the house of God, men and women were segregated. Matches were made by parents and elders, not by young lovers. Compatibility was determined by financial and social status, work ethic, and overall character, not by a meeting of the eyes or the spark ignited by a first kiss. A prospective bride's value was gauged by how much her family could offer in the way of a dowry, and a groom's value hinged on his ability to provide for a family. Both were expected to be God-fearing, respectful of traditions, and obedient toward their elders.

George had sullied her reputation, but there was still a chance he might choose to marry her—as he had promised. The men in her family, Panayota knew, would be duty-bound to make sure he did exactly that. Her only other choice was to recede into the shadows and hope that people might one day forget, or at least forgive, her indiscretions. Otherwise, she would carry the shame of her illicit romance for the rest of her life.

It was nearly midnight when Panayota finally decided to respond to her cousin. Pursing her lips together, she whistled just loud enough to be heard by Aggelo above her.

She was tired of hiding. She was tired of keeping secrets.

———⋄———

See end of book for **Index of Names** of the people mentioned in this story. Also, on pages 68-72 there are useful **topographic photos**.

———⋄———

CHAPTER 3:
MARRIED OR TARNISHED

LIKE EVERYTHING ELSE IN THE region, the village of Kupaki sat on a hillside and was surrounded in every direction by more craggy hills and mountains as high as 9,000 feet. The village boasted no straight lines, no flat ground. Isolated in a picturesque landscape of rolling hills and rugged scrubland, a lonely outpost above a river far below, it was a world unto itself.

The two main cobble stone paths dissected the village like a cross, the lines converging at the main square in the middle of the village. The houses were made of gray stone and had a balcony overlooking the terraced village, roof tiles the color of burnt sienna, two bedrooms, one or two fireplaces, a living room, and a kitchen. There was no running water and no electricity in any of the homes.

The most important public buildings were the church and school that stood next to each other at the lower part of the village, visible from nearly every house.

News and the gossip for the three hundred permanent residents, who supported themselves by farming and shepherding sheep or goats, were exchanged by the men mostly at the general village stores which stood around the village public square, and by the women at the water springs, the bigger of which was near the middle of the village and several smaller ones at the peripheral neighborhoods.

Kupaki was nearly inscrutable at night, a murky tableau of mystery and shadow, but in the light of day, the tiny village held

11

no secrets. Everybody knew everybody and secrets, even intimate in nature were nearly impossible to be upheld. A stranger stood out and rumors spread like wildfire.

As Thanasis pondered his cousin's dilemma, he did so with her family, her neighbors, and the village itself in mind. The men in the family wanted to force George to marry Panayota, but the women thought she should absorb the shame of their illicit affair now and forget about the young man, who would most likely make her miserable for the rest of her life. Better to endure a few whispers and disapproving stares now, they said, than to marry a scoundrel. Common sense told Thanasis that the women were right, but his pride told him something else.

A few days later, when he spotted George walking near the village store, Thanasis hastened his steps to catch up with the young man. George had been avoiding him, but Thanasis was determined to confront him. He would try to make peace, but if no solution presented itself, he was prepared to show his teeth.

"George," Thanasis said, "you know and I know what's happened with Panayota. I want you to honor your word."

Before George could reply, much less digest Thanasis's words, James approached from the nearby vineyards. "Hi," he said as soon as he joined them.

George acknowledged James and then turned to Thanasis. "There is nothing going on between me and Panayota. Do not listen to the village gossip."

"Leave that out," Thanasis snapped. "We know better."

James spoke up. "George, I treated you as a friend, and you came near me and my home. At the end, you slept with my sister and blemished her honor. All the family is against me now. I'll give my sister seventy thousand drachmas as a dowry. I don't want you to feel you're marrying James's sister without a dowry. I'll support my sister and be a very good brother to you."

George glanced away thoughtfully. "I need to think it over," he said. "I have sisters who aren't married yet. I want to be a good, protective brother and wait to marry until after they have married."

"What do you mean?" Thanasis retorted. "Some of your sisters are several years younger than you. Are you going to take decisions when they are of marriageable age?"

George looked like prey trying to squirm free from a predator's jaws. "I have no job. I might need to leave the village. I might have to go to America all together. I have not promised anything to Panayota, anyway."

James's young, innocent-looking face darkened. "Why, you two-faced fuck..."

Thanasis, moving a step closer, locked eyes with George. "Listen, you had better honor your word to my cousin. I will not let that honor be lost to you. I will see that you forget all these excuses and think hard on solutions."

Thanasis could intimidate and even threaten George. Panayota, on the other hand, he had to treat far more gently.

He had always felt protective of his cousin, whose family, he felt, had already borne a great hardship. Panayota's father, had died only a few years after crossing the Atlantic in search of his fortune, one among a million young Greek men to immigrate to America between 1910 and 1920. Already the father of two girls, he had left determined to build a new life for his family. But unbeknownst to him, he had already created a new life, and that life was growing in his wife's womb. He never met his son. James was just four years old when news arrived that his father, a phantom he only knew through stories, photos, and letters, had died in surgery, the victim of stomach troubles.

From that day on, Panayota's family had been forced to think about just one thing: survival. The fields they owned in the village produced barely enough food for the family, so, the eldest sister went to work for other villagers in their fields for daily wages. She also found work as a seamstress when no one needed her in the fields. Panayota was hired by a neighboring family, that looked after her like one of their own. James, Skevi's baby, was doted on by his mother. If he got so much as an upset stomach, she teetered on the edge of panic. Understandably so, Thanasis thought, given how his father had died.

As the days wore on after Panayota's second virginity test, Thanasis spoke with her repeatedly, often for hours at a time, but she had a mind of her own.

"What about... ?"

Each time she began a sentence that way, Thanasis knew his cousin was about to invoke the name of some young man in the village who had gone from troublemaker to domesticated husband in a few short years.

"Was he a saint?" she would ask. "Was he not immature?"

She would then refer to specific incidents known by all in the village, incidents that revealed the young man's colorful past.

"Isn't he a good family man today?" she would ask.

Thanasis couldn't deny her logic, but at the same time he knew George belonged to a different breed. He was like a wild animal: cagey and unpredictable. Could anyone tame him? Even now, as the village buzzed with the rumors of his tawdry behavior, he regularly walked the path by her boss's home, singing or whispering little love songs he had composed while Panayota was at work. Or he would stand on the balcony of his home, from where Panayota's house was visible, and, feigning innocence, invoke an old Greek tune:

> *Come to your window*
> *And out of sight from your mom.*
> *And pretend that you are watering*
> *The pot with marjoram.*

Finally, one day a solution presented itself. Thanasis was just leaving a cousin's home next door to the Nitsoses when George's mother, called to him.

"Are you just going to stand there in the street, Thanasis?" she asked in a friendly voice. "Or would you like to come in and have a thimble of ouzo with me?"

Thanasis gladly accepted the invitation, and once inside, he only waited as long as politeness dictated before broaching the topic foremost on his mind.

"Aunt," he began, pausing to take a sip of the sugary, anise-flavored aperitif George's mother had given him, "Your family and our family have always had good relations. I don't want to do anything to change that, but you should know what has happened between George and Panayota."

"I know," she answered with a perceptive nod. "I know the whole story."

"Then you know what that means for a girl in our village," Thanasis replied. "My cousin is tarnished."

She frowned thoughtfully. "I know. I have girls myself, but listen, I don't want you and your family to worry. George is going to do the right thing by Panayota. He was always going to."

Thanasis cocked his head in surprise. He had no reason to doubt George's mother. If she was right, then Panayota's problem—the family's problem—was solved at last.

CHAPTER 4:
OMEN

PANAYOTA SMILED TO HERSELF AS the little convoy was approaching Kupaki. Just ahead of her were a couple of muleteers. Walking behind them with another mule was George Nitsos, her gallant fiancé, followed by several other muleteers.

Five years had passed since her cousin Thanasis had sat down to sip ouzo with George's mother, and in that time, George and Panayota had enjoyed a long, uneventful engagement. True, they had never hosted an official engagement party, but they had nevertheless won the grudging approval of their families and village. Soon they would be wed at St. George's Church.

At the moment, they were crossing a bridge over a river in the heat of the noon-day sun and inching closer to home. They'd left a port by the sea earlier that morning, their dowry packed and loaded by mule drivers in anticipation of the slow trek back to Kupaki, which would cover more than twenty miles and take all day. Weighing down their procession of pack mules was an assortment of bedding, chests, silverware, plates, napkins, towels, and tablecloths—a remarkable haul purchased with their combined finances. Like any other young couple, they had relied on their family's wealth as well as their own meager resources, including Panayota's earnings from working for her neighbors. Thanks to Panayota's savings and the money sent from George's father in America, they'd been able to spend a princely sum, which in turn had earned them a bonus gift: a magnificent set of glassware from the store owner in the big city near the sea.

The gift, as dictated by custom, had been directly proportional to the amount of money they had spent. Unwilling to trust the beautiful glassware's fate to any of the muleteers, George had insisted on carrying it on the mule he was leading.

Panayota could see the future already. She and George would entertain often, sharing their home and their bounty with the same people who had once threatened to chop her into pieces and toss her into the river. She would savor the delicious irony of her newfound domestic status as she poured each of her guests a refreshing drink from an exquisite glass pitcher. "More water?" she could imagine saying. "It's fresh from the—"

A terrible crash behind her—then the sound of George shouting in alarm—jolted her from her reverie. She turned to see him standing beside his mule and staring angrily at the ground where the box containing the prized glassware lay on its side. Judging by the percussive sound generated by its impact, the glassware was in pieces.

"Fuck the fucking box and the fucking glassware!" a red-faced George snarled. His charming smile had disappeared, and his mischievous eyes were no longer dancing. "Fuck its father! Fuck its mother!"

Panayota covered her mouth with her hand. Should she laugh or cry? She wasn't sure. Finally, she decided to open the box, just to see with her own eyes that indeed her lovely glassware was no more. But before she could take hold of the lid, George jerked her away.

"Just let the fucking thing lie there!" he spat out.

Panayota glanced from her fuming fiancé to the other muleteers, who were looking away in embarrassment. She felt a growing sense of foreboding. Was this to be her future? If so, it frightened her.

On June 2, 1940, as everyone gathered at St. George's Church, Thanasis glanced from pew to pew and saw that nearly the entire village had come to watch Papazois, the village priest, bless the union of George and Panayota. Although he'd pushed George to do the right thing by Panayota, Thanasis sometimes wondered if the women in the family had been wiser: maybe he should have let the scoundrel off the hook. Dressed in his best suit and wearing a look of self-satisfaction, the lean groom looked like the proverbial cat that had just swallowed the canary.

A man in his shoes should exercise more humility, Thanasis thought.

After all, George Nitsos was about to commit his life to another soul in front of God and everyone he knew. Thanasis knew from experience that such a commitment could not be rushed into—or taken lightly. He himself was engaged now to Polyxeni Gumas, a good friend and former classmate of Panayota's. Their engagement, he reflected, was the result of patience and negotiation, not hubris.

A year earlier, while still an eligible bachelor, Thanasis had been approached by the village store owner and Polyxeni's uncle, who had suggested that Thanasis consider marrying his niece. Negotiations, however, had quickly broken down when Thanasis's father, began insisting on a larger dowry than the Gumas family could provide. Panayota became one of Polyxeni's most vocal proponents, citing the girl's beauty, work ethic, and academic achievement. "She herself is the dowry," Panayota told Thanasis. Thanasis's father continued to insist on a more substantial dowry. It wasn't long before he had earned the nickname of "Dowry Konandreas," as well as the moniker, "Gave dowry, will have dowry," which was often chanted by the younger generation of Gumases as soon as he was out of earshot and followed by howls of mirth.

There was also the matter of Thanasis's reputation—and Polyxeni's view of him. He had made a disastrous impression, years earlier, when he had beaten up another man and the news had reached his father—and Polyxeni and her family—while the group had been talking at a market in a nearby town. Worse, there was his thundering voice. He was loud. His whole family was loud. They had to be in order to communicate out in the fields. Such rough edges weren't exactly a selling point when it came to seeking out a potential bride.

Thanasis's sisters and their husbands had told him that Polyxeni was a very nice young maiden, but since each husband's family had received a hefty dowry from the Konandreases, they had hesitated to say a dowry shouldn't be an issue. Panayota, though, had possessed no dowry when she had been courted by George. She had acted on her own and in fact had disregarded many village and family biases. Thus, when Thanasis had all but given up on the idea of marrying Polyxeni, Panayota had reminded him privately that it was his decision to get married, not his father's. Thanasis had countered that he didn't want to disregard his parents' opinions, at which point his cousin had cleverly pointed out that his father only disapproved of the dowry, not the girl. Marrying Polyxeni would not be the same thing as disregarding his father's wishes. Thanasis had finally presented the argument to his parents in simple terms: "Polyxeni is better than a thousand dowries." His father, impressed by his son's earnest plea, had capitulated.

Thanasis glanced from George Nitsos, still looking smug at the altar, to his fiancée. Indeed, Polyxeni Gumas was worth more than any dowry. One of the most beautiful women inside the church, she exuded equal parts dignity and calm. She was a force to be reckoned with, and he could hardly wait for their turn at the altar.

He got it two months later when, on August 23, 1940, they exchanged their own wedding vows. Soon after, his father was singing the praises of his new daughter-in-law, who was hardworking, obedient, and gentle. In fact, it seemed there were few qualities that Polyxeni did not possess for Thanasis's father. He extolled her virtues with the same passion he had employed while arguing against the marriage.

CHAPTER 5:
WAR AND DANCING

BY OCTOBER 1940, THE HILLS surrounding Kupaki were aflame in autumnal shades of red, silver, yellow, and green. Chrysanthemums, geraniums, and quince fruit adorned front yards, balconies, and gardens. That was the last Thanasis would see of his village or its blooms until the following year.

Greece, bullied and provoked by Italy, was about to enter World War II. Thanasis would be among Kupaki's thirty-five young men, including George Nitsos, to leave the village and join the fighting in the mountains to the north. The lesser equipped Greek army trounced the Italians, but then Hitler sent his elite German troops to the region to attack Greece on several fronts. After a heroic resistance effort, Greece was eventually forced to surrender.

The German occupation of Greece entered its darkest days. Germans confiscated food supplies to use for their own soldiers and allies, as well as their expedition to Africa. The occupants also enforced a blockade, preventing food from being imported or even shipped from one part of Greece, where it was produced to another. Locally, several villagers died from malnutrition and poor medical care. The Konandreas and Gumas families, like most in Kupaki, endured their share of misfortune. By the end of 1943, Thanasis and Polyxeni had each lost their father.

The blockade forced many families to move from the big cities to the countryside in order to find enough food to survive. The poor mountainous villages around Kupaki were now experiencing an influx of former residents, many of whom had not been seen in the villages for decades.

These young returnees were direct descendants of shepherds, derisively called *Galatades*-Milk Men – by the Athenians, who since 1920 had been undertaking an annual winter sojourn to Athens. Each family would gather their flock in October and walk for seventeen days straight, all the way to Athens. Once in the capital city, they would settle on the foothills around the city, sleeping in primitive shacks. During the day, they would sell milk and other dairy products to the parliamentary elite Athenians. Then, in early spring, they would walk back to the village. The Galatades' exposure to such privileged Athenians taught them how to appreciate the finer things in life, things they didn't have: education, and material possessions such as nice clothing and jewelry. Along with their milk money, they were bringing back to the village new styles of dress, openly flaunting them.

On this return, however, there was no time for a show, as the newcomers immediately got to work plowing, digging, and planting. Most bought or had been given by the locals one or two goats for their milk.

George Nitsos was ecstatic to see all the young people return, and soon he was interacting with them on a daily basis.

In time, the old-timers were able to appreciate the educational opportunities the big city had given to the newcomers, but they were less impressed by their urban moral codes which were looser and more individualistic. Kupaki, isolated for so many years by its rugged hills and remote location, struggled to hold back the tides of modernization.

Thanasis learned that the youth of the village, organized by the newcomers, had joined a youth resistance movement and had prepared a theatrical performance with resistance themes. A dance followed in the open behind the altar at St. George and was enjoyed by all.

A few days later, Thanasis was returning with Polyxeni one

night from their field when he noticed several people standing in a group in the street looking into the school's big hall. He stopped his horse and could hear the voices of George Nitsos and Tsipanos from inside the building.

"What is it?" Polyxeni asked.

Two main paths converged behind the school hall, and others had stopped as well to take in the spectacle. Farmers and shepherds, tired from working all day in the fields, paused alongside their horses and mules to see what was happening. Some of the older men and women on hand were crossing themselves in disbelief. Others were shaking their heads in disapproval.

Polyxeni gulped. "Are they ... dancing?"

Thanasis raised an eyebrow. "I'm not sure I'd call that dancing."

"Who is teaching them this thing?" Polyxeni asked.

Thanasis, unsure, shrugged his shoulders.

"They have a dance instructor," answered a young bystander, who appeared knowledgeable on the subject. "Your cousin Tsipanos knows him and brought him here to teach dancing."

"Oh, crazy Tsipanos," Polyxeni murmured.

A conversation ensued between Thanasis, Polyxeni, the young bystander, and several others, and Thanasis was slowly brought up to speed on the dancing. The instructor was Nick, who hailed from a village north of Kupaki. He had learned the European dances at a studio in Athens, dancing in the evenings after working all day. To most congregating outside the school hall, Nick was a stranger and an outsider who had left his village and his work in his fields and come to Kupaki to teach a new dance. Tsipanos, Polyxeni's cousin and a young theology student, had recently returned to Kupaki from the University of Athens. After the theater dance, he had realized that the youth in his village were out of step with their cosmopolitan counterparts and had asked Nick, whom he knew, to come to the village, stay at his place, and bring the latest European dances to Kupaki.

"Is he doing it for free?" Polyxeni asked.

22

Money, thanks to the war, was no longer worth anything, and people bartered for what they wanted.

"The students will pay him in wheat," the same young man answered.

At the sound of the word wheat, many crossed themselves. Money was worth nothing, but wheat was precious.

For his part, Thanasi wanted nothing to do with the madness. He was old enough to know that such behavior rubbed the villagers the wrong way. Their country was occupied. Their people were starving, and the youth wanted to learn a new dance and pay with wheat?

The next evening, Thanasis spotted more curious villagers gathered around the school. A gramophone inside was blaring a tune completely different from the traditional regional melodies.

Thanasis had learned the latest gossip about the dancing from his wife's siblings, three of whom were in the class. They had argued with their mother Aliki, by saying that the dance had attracted almost forty students and that there was nothing wrong with it. They had pointed out that it was their cousin Tsipanos who had organized it, and brought Nick to the village.

Aliki had already expressed her frustration directly to Tsipanos, the young theology student, for his role in what to her was a scandal.

"You left the village for Athens to study God," she told her nephew Tsipanos, "and you brought the devil back with you." The devil, of course, was Nick, the dance instructor.

The village's youth had argued that it wasn't just young people participating; some married couples, like George and Panayota, were attending the classes, as well. George, in fact, was urging everybody to participate. With even married couples joining in, Thanasis was now convinced, no one could stop the dancing. Life would go on, with or without money, with or without enough food on the table. The youth of the village would see to that. What Thanasis couldn't understand was what George and Panayota were doing there?

At half past four every afternoon, young men and women

abandoned their work in droves. Their parents would take over for them while they rushed home to change. On their way home, the girls would stop at the springs to wash their hands, feet, and armpits. The more enterprising among them would perfume themselves with basil leaves from their gardens or a rose from the school's flower garden, mashing the plants into a pulp in their hands and rubbing the paste into their armpits or around their necks.

Like the others in attendance, George and Panayota had paid the price of admission, which was good for the summer: two okas (ten pounds) of wheat for her and three okas (fifteen pounds) for him. The dance, meanwhile, was like nothing anyone had ever seen. The older generation didn't even bother to learn how to pronounce the names of—much less differentiate between— of the new dances. Whether it was a tango, waltz, or fox trot, the old-timers dismissively called it *Kolito,* or fusion, since it hardly resembled traditional Greek line dancing. The new dances, which paired couples in close proximity, came to be synonymous with sinfulness and licentiousness. Men and women held hands and moved closely together, simultaneously insulting common morals, culture, and tradition. Parents, grandparents, and other elders in town were incredulous that the youth in the village were so willing to give away good wheat during a near famine just to prance around the hall, but their protests were to no avail.

A few days after the first dance lesson, Thanasis and Polyxeni met Panayota outside the school hall.

"You're such a good dancer, cousin," Thanasis said disapprovingly. "These lessons are a waste for you. It's time you concentrate on other things that need attention, like having children."

Panayota offered a self-deprecating smile. "Oh, Thanasis, you know what a big baby George is. I'm not sure I could handle having another child in the family."

Thanasis laughed politely.

"Anyway," Panayota continued, "George needs my company here. I have to keep an eye on him, don't I? One of the graceful young things inside might have designs on my husband." She broke into a peal of laughter that belied the dangerous truth in her words.

Thanasis shook his head glumly. When Panayota made up her mind to do something, there was no dissuading her.

The dancing sessions ran late each night, and Panayota was surprised one evening when the old hand-wound clock on the school wall struck ten o'clock. The dancers were illuminated by a flickering kerosene lamp, which cast long shadows of figures on the walls. Beyond the windows, shapes could be spied in the darkness outside, where parents waiting to escort their children back home stood alongside curious onlookers. Many were moving to the music. They would be fresh converts for Nick, Panayota mused.

Inside the hall, Panayota noticed her husband dancing with a buxom young girl whose flushed cheeks were doing nothing to dissuade her partner from calling out endearments to her. Such behavior wasn't new for George, who regularly began the night dancing with cousins before moving on to other young ladies not related to him by blood. His vulgar flirtations invariably embarrassed the girls, but he always had a ready excuse for treating them so familiarly.

"Now, George, please!" the girl said, pushing his hand away when he squeezed her and bent over as if to kiss her.

George feigned innocence. "Come on now. We're like family. My great-uncle's sister-in-law was your father's ..."

Panayota leaned against the back wall and tried her best not to acknowledge her husband's shameful conduct. It was going to be another long night.

The song came to an end, and Nick reached for the gramophone's needle to remove it from the record, which was still spinning.

George, ever impetuous, availed himself of the brief lull. "Any of you young guys want to take my wife?" he asked, laughing.

"It won't be for nothing. I will make sure she comes with a good dowry."

The room fell silent, and, judging by the look on George's face, he quickly understood that he had gone too far.

Panayota glanced around the room nervously. "Don't worry, George," she said, flashing a smile. "You won't have to give anybody a dowry. All these young men know what a lady like me is worth. They'll be happy to have me for nothing."

George, clearly hoping to make amends for his crude remark, was quick to reply. "Don't I know that, my sweet?" he said in the sugary voice that so many women in the village seemed to find irresistible. "Looks like you're the only one here that knows I was joking. Look at all their faces! Do you all really think I would give up my darling wife? Not for a million drachmas! Not for the whole world!"

A few days later, George sat down with the dance instructor to enjoy a glass of ouzo. George couldn't help relishing the fact that someone else—Nick in this case—was bearing the brunt of the village's scorn. Several elders regularly cursed Nick and prayed for the day he would leave the village and never come back. They complained that never before had young unmarried men and women been in such close proximity to each other, which could only lead to trouble. They complained that the young people not only spent precious time and wheat on learning to dance but had also begun practicing dance steps while working in the fields.

"Do you know that you and I are not just spreading licentiousness in Kupaki?" George quipped. "We're also to blame for bad crops and lost sheep."

Nick laughed quietly as he sipped at his ouzo.

The dance lessons had become the talk of the village. Who was carrying on with whom? Who smelled strongly of basil and sweat? Whose wheat was justifiably spent? And whose was simply wasted because he had two left feet?

Panayota came to dread dance lessons. There was no telling

who George was going to flirt with or what he was going to say on any given night. How would he embarrass her next? By now, many were openly gossiping about his designs on Poly, a pretty young girl who showed up each night at the dance hall. He was dancing with her over and over, whispering in her ear. His demeanor was showing utmost infatuation, but because Panayota was there and Poly was the granddaughter of his godfather, few suspected George's true intentions toward Poly.

The afternoon of August 29, 1944, Panayota's worries were overshadowed by the occupation as she watched in disbelief plumes of roiling black smoke rising in the east over the hill of St. Nicholas. The Germans, determined to punish the resistance for an ambush earlier in the month near the county's capital, burned the town to the ground.

The other villagers who had arrived for the nightly dance lesson searched the horizon nervously. Several turned and started for home, disappearing behind the stately cypress and poplar trees that lined the schoolyard.

George remained defiant. He strode into the school hall and began turning the crank on the gramophone. "Let's have one more glass!" he called out to the others. "One more red one!"

Kakia Mendris's popular song extolling the pleasures of "one more glass, one more song" blared jovially from the gramophone: *"Akoma ena potiraki, Akoma ena tragudaki ... "*

"Come on, everybody!" George continued. "Cheer up! If we're all going to die, we might as well die dancing!"

Panayota did not know then how close Kupaki and the next villages were to such retaliation by the Germans. It came to light later. At Krokylion, the village less than three miles from Kupaki, the leftists were hiding Elias Barzilai, the chief Rabbi of the Jewish Community of Athens, along with his wife and teenage daughter. And at another village, less than two miles from Kupaki, all the records with the names of all the Jews of Athens were hidden. Information of this sort would have brought the Germans, torches and guns in hand.

The dance lessons, meanwhile, came to an end a few days

later. Nick had managed to amass one hundred and seventy okas of wheat, enough to feed a family of four frugally for nearly six months. He loaded the sacks onto two horses and set off, stopping at a villager's house on the way out of the village to return the gramophone he had borrowed, along with seventeen okas of wheat as payment.

Kupaki's youth missed him before he even disappeared from view. Even some adults who had vehemently criticized him lamented his departure. "For all his prancing and turning the heads of our children," some said, "that lad wasn't so bad, after all."

Panayota, too, was sad to see him leave, but she also felt a sense of relief. The nightly roulette with George and his crude remarks from the center of the school hall—for everyone to hear—was over.

CHAPTER 6:
FLIRTING

It wasn't long before Panayota's public humiliation was old news, for the villagers soon had something new to talk about: the German occupiers were packing up their trucks and leaving. The locals reacted by cursing the withdrawing Germans within earshot. Those who had lost loved ones to the fighting were especially vocal.

While the Germans headed for the exit, one man, now a hero, was rumored to be returning. Nick, it was said, was planning to marry one of his ex-students. The village buzzed with anticipation. Soon Nick and his young bride would be elegantly performing the Dance of Isaiah, a much-venerated ritual at any Greek Orthodox wedding, at St. George Church.

Along with the news about Nick's plans, another rumor was spreading in the village about George's latest infatuation: Poly, granddaughter of his godfather. Though the dancing at the school's hall was over, he was wasting no opportunity to besiege her, and there were plenty of opportunities.

The weather during the 1944 autumn harvest was glorious, with one sunny day following another. The grain and grape harvests, the husking, the wine and syrup making, the fruit picking—all were occasions for merrymaking, courtship, and dancing to gramophone music. During the dancing, many times in the open with the villagers looking on, George had been seen whispering endearments to Poly with impunity.

Panayota tried to tell herself that even George would not be so godless as to taint a relationship by baptism, but she could see that he was becoming bolder still.

In the days that followed, the rumors continued to spread, with each one eventually finding its way to Panayota's ears. George was passing messages to Poly now. He was rendezvousing with her outside the village in remote places where they had no earthly reason to meet.

Panayota briefly considered confronting her husband. After all, she knew his pattern all too well. This was how he had courted her not so long ago—secretly and without the village's approval. If she confronted him, she knew he would simply go on the offensive. He would pretend to be shocked.

She could see his reaction now:

"How could you even consider the possibility of such a relationship?"

Perhaps, had George possessed a better work ethic, he would have been too busy for such dalliances. After the Germans left and Greece was officially liberated, the country undertook a great rebuilding effort with the help of foreign aid. Suddenly American dollars were pouring into the country. George, who quit his job as the village warden as soon as his father began sending money again, boasted to anyone who would listen about his sudden influx of wealth. Much of that money was spent on his wardrobe, which he carefully cultivated as part of his urban veneer. Always dressed to the nines, he spent most of his time loafing about in the village square, where he endeavored to impress his fellow villagers with card tricks and the streetwise language he had adopted during his youthful days in the big city of Patras.

The pressure to do something—anything—to stop George from continuing his pursuit of Poly reached a fever pitch one day when Thanasis was approached by Mary, the wife of a poor shepherd, while at his fields.

"Linatsas," she said, using George's nickname, "told me he's planning to divorce Panayota, so he can marry Poly."

Thanasis felt his blood boil. He had already discussed the issue with Polyxeni, Aggelo, and his other sister Papadia, who had insisted that he take the matter to Poly's father. Aggelo, in fact, had already approached Panayota, who had denied the rumors and attributed them to malicious gossip. Thanasis had at first resisted the idea of confronting Poly's father, who was his distant cousin.

Yet here was Mary, not known as a gossip, confirming what everyone suspected. How could he not get involved?

Thanasis thanked Mary for her candor and then marched straight to his cousin's house.

"I knew George was after my daughter," Poly's father said in an alarmed tone after Thanasis told him what George was doing, "but I had no idea he was actually planning on divorcing Panayota. I'm going to have a long talk with Poly."

A few weeks later, Thanasis met again with Poly's father after it had become apparent that his talk had not produced the desired results. George was still inventing ways to get close to her.

"I will either have to leave the village with her," Poly's father said, "or kill the bastard."

Thanasis raised a hand in protest. "Don't even think such things," he said, remembering a time not so long in the past when he had spent time in jail after losing his temper.

Thanasis breathed a sigh of relief that summer when George received a government appointment to a city farther north in Greece. There he was to receive military training along with many others and, if judged fit, to be utilized by the Nationalists in the war against the Communists. Despite his best efforts to play both sides, George Nitsos had been forced to come down squarely on the side of the Nationalists. Whether or not he would be able to maintain loyalty to anyone but himself was a matter very much open to debate.

CHAPTER 7:
SHINING STAR OF THE SKY

PANAYOTA WAS WALKING A WINDING cobblestone path near her home one sunny morning in early September 1946 when she heard a familiar echo. The mailman was announcing his arrival in Kupaki by blowing his curved brass horn. Judging by the percussive rebound of the proclamation as it sliced its way along the village's narrow footpaths, the mailman was almost to the village square. Although he only came to Kupaki two or three times each week, usually around ten o'clock in the morning, he almost always had something for Panayota, who regularly received letters from her various family members in America, New Zealand, Australia, and, closer to home, Athens. These days, she could also count on a letter from George each week now that he was away.

That day, however, Panayota didn't have her own mail in mind. Her hands tingled with dread and her heart raced as she scurried down the path. She reached the village square just as several others were converging on it from other directions.

Ahead was the mailman, horn still in hand, bulging leather bag slung over his shoulder. As a growing crowd began to gather around the frail, thin man, he climbed the stone steps from the main square to the front of the village store that was his final destination. The mailman, assuming an air of importance, placed his leather bag on a metal tripod table and sat on a chair beside it. He seemed pleased that so many had assembled around him.

Indeed, Panayota noted there were more on hand than usual, most likely because of the summer vacation.

The mailman was slowly and deliberately removing various items from the many compartments in his leather bag: stamps, a fountain pen, a small bottle of ink, wax to seal envelopes, his old wrinkled logbook, and finally the mail itself. He was obviously savoring each moment, basking in his importance, as the circle of villagers around him drew closer.

She took up a position directly behind the mail man, so she could gaze over his bony left shoulder as he began reading out the names on the envelopes and packages.

It was all Panayota could do to quell the impatience welling up inside her. She watched intently as he began to call out the names of each recipient one letter at a time. When she spied the name, she had been looking for, she snatched the letter from the mailman before he could read for himself the name on the envelope, much less announce it to the assembled crowd.

A speechless mailman jerked around in surprise.

"I'll deliver that for you," Panayota said breezily. "It's for my husband's cousin. He's still in his fields and has asked me to collect his mail."

The mailman nodded his assent, although a look of surprise still showed on his face. He might have protested, Panayota thought, if she had ever given him a reason to suspect her motives. In the past, she'd only had honest dealings with him. Moreover, in such a close-knit community, it was quite common, even necessary, for the postman to allow villagers to pass on letters to their friends and family.

With the letter safely tucked beneath her arm, Panayota hurried across the slate-covered yard of the store and disappeared around the corner. Once out of sight, she continued halfway home and then stopped where the path curved between houses. With shaking hands she tore the letter from the envelope. As her eyes raced down the page, she unconsciously formed each word with her lips. By the time she had finished the letter, she was blind with rage.

She jerked around violently and stormed back the way she had come.

Seconds later, she was back on the path next to the store. The mailman, still seated beside the metal table, was placidly licking stamps for the outgoing mail while sipping ouzo offered by one of the villagers, probably someone who had just received good news. Panayota marched straight past him and stopped in the middle of the village square facing Poly's house. In the middle of the square and in front of dozens of her fellow villagers, a panting and furious Panayota vented her spleen.

"Come out, you!" she called toward Poly's house. "Come out and hear what your darling has written to you!"

As she began to read from the letter in her trembling hand, Panayota barely noticed the others in the square, the store, the balconies, and the paths who had collectively stopped whatever they'd been doing—reading, making small talk, relaxing in the shade—to stare at her.

"My very beloved Poly, shining star of the sky..." Panayota's voice was choked with fury.

The letter she had stolen wasn't addressed to George's cousin, of course. It was for Poly—and had been written by George.

The mailman leapt to his feet, nearly stumbling in the process, ouzo trickling down the side of his mouth, and rushed down the stone steps. "Stop!" he called out to Panayota as he waved his arms wildly. "Stop reading! I'm going to lose my job! I'm going to lose my job!"

His small, squeaky voice was no match for Panayota's full-throated recitation of her husband's amorous dispatch to Poly. She continued reading the letter aloud for all to hear until finally, exhausted from her exertions, she suddenly became aware of the mailman, who was still pleading with her to stop. Panayota felt her cheeks pale. What had she done? To steal someone else's mail, to possibly jeopardize an innocent man's job—this was not like her.

"I'm sorry," she said softly. She then raised her voice, so her audience could hear. "He has done nothing wrong. If it ever comes to him losing his job, I will own up to my responsibility and tell any official that will listen that I snatched this letter from his hands and ran away."

A few short days later, Poly's father left the village with his daughter in tow. His dark prediction—that he might someday have to leave his home in order to preserve his family's honor—had come to fruition much sooner than anyone could have anticipated.

Thanasis was proud of his cousin's spirit, although he feared for her safety. How would that cowardly philanderer react when news reached him that Poly had been whisked away by her father after Panayota had aired their dirty secrets for all to hear? Panayota would never leave George; she was too honorable, but what about him? Would he find a way to pay her back for standing up to him?

Only a handful of days had passed since Panayota's furious recitation in the village square. The sultry summer weather was still hanging on, although the September days were growing shorter. At the moment, Thanasis was standing on the second floor of the Konandreas' hut, a rustic building in the middle of the family's fields, just outside of Kupaki. Hay and other livestock supplies were stored on the first floor, while the second level, an open space, was meant for family living quarters. A fireplace occupied the far wall and sat opposite the east-facing balcony.

Across from Thanasis stood Takis and Mary. Takis, a hardy peasant farmer barely five feet four inches tall, was illiterate, but an accomplished cooper and the owner of a keen, philosophical mind. He was always inquisitive about how things worked and how nature functioned. His wife was perhaps an inch shorter. Lean, hard of hearing, she, too, was illiterate but sharp.

Together, they had just made an explosive allegation: George Nitsos, before leaving for military training, had not once, but several times offered to pay them to kill Panayota.

35

Takis and Mary worked in George's fields as crop partners and were dependent upon him for their livelihood. They were simple, hardworking, God-fearing people, who had just told Thanasis their story which he found incredible.

"Takis, are you sure you heard, right?" Thanasis asked.

"Which part of George Nitsos offering us money to kill Panayota could we have heard wrong?" Takis replied.

"I might be a bit hard of hearing," his wife Mary added, "but I heard it very well—and many times, indeed."

"Tell me again how he approached you," he said.

"We thought he was joking at first," Mary explained. "He asked us if we would help kill Panayota. He said she had some illness in her womb that meant she could never have children. We said she looked well enough to us, and even if she was ill, surely modern doctors could cure her. We told him she's still young and can get better and have children."

"That's when he said he wanted to get rid of her so he could marry Poly," Takis said. "He talked like he was joking, but we could tell he was dead serious."

"How exactly did he want you to do it?" Thanasis asked.

"He wanted me to call her from outside the house," Takis said, "and throw a hand grenade at her when she came out. Nitsos said that everybody would think that she was just at the wrong place at the wrong time when the guerillas and the royalists were throwing grenades at each other."

As he listened to his explanation, Thanasis wondered why Takis and his wife had waited so long to tell him about George's plans. But then it dawned on him: it was possible they had kept the conspiracy a secret from him for precisely the same reason he was currently doubting his own resolve to tell anyone else: no one would believe it.

"I managed to get out of it by saying that I had no idea how to use a grenade," Takis continued. "He offered to teach me, but I said that I was too old a dog to learn new tricks. Another day, he came early one morning and said that he had arranged things so that Panayota would be riding to meet him there later that day and we should surprise her horse when she arrived at that steep part of the path where there's an eighty-foot drop on one side. He said she would fall all the way to the bottom head-first."

"And how did you get out of that one?"

"He was there, too, hiding behind a rock with Mary's kerchief covering his head so his wife wouldn't recognize him even if she saw him. When Panayota appeared about a hundred yards away, I told him that I could hear people coming in the opposite direction. He just leapt up and ran away before she got too close."

Thanasis frowned in disgust. "I can't believe that," he muttered.

Takis wasn't finished. "He offered us money, clothing, a house to live in, livestock—you name it. He even talked about pushing her from an oak tree so that the fall would kill her."

"I'll have to talk to Panayota about this," Thanasis said, thinking aloud as he began to pace the wide plank flooring.

"I already did," Mary said sheepishly.

"What?" Thanasis couldn't believe his ears. "What else have you been hiding from me?"

Takis nervously eyed the bare ceiling joists above them before returning Thanasis's gaze. "There was another time," he finally said, "when Nitsos asked me to help his cousin kill Panayota when she would be on her way to their fields. I went to see her before she was going to depart with my heart in my mouth. I told her not to go to her fields, and I pleaded with her not to talk to her husband about it and get me in trouble."

"And how did she react?"

"She burst into tears," he said, "and I consoled her, telling her that nobody would blame her if she divorced him, because we all know how he treats her. After a while, she dried her tears and made me promise not to tell anyone else in return for her not telling her husband what I'd told her."

"And she still hasn't divorced him!" Thanasis said in wonder.

Mary shrugged. "She told me, 'Don't talk to me about divorce, Mary. I would rather be dead than be the only divorced

37

woman in the village.' And she asked me to leave before Nitsos returned."

"You do realize, don't you," Thanasis said to the old couple, "that I can't just let this go. I'll have to talk to Panayota, and she will know you told me."

They nodded.

"We are not among those people with loose tongues," Mary said. "But if it saves that poor woman's life, may the good Lord forgive us for talking to you against her wishes, even if she herself does not."

"Amen," Takis said. "Please be careful. If Nitsos finds out, we won't have a roof over our heads, and we may be the ones lying dead in a ravine somewhere."

After the couple departed, Thanasis's mind raced. If George had truly asked such a thing of the Takis and Mary, it was only because he felt confident they were too dependent on him for work to ever go against him. As poor as they were, perhaps he thought they would do his bidding—if the price was right. By speaking almost in jest, he could always claim he was joking, should things go awry.

Thanasis briefly contemplated confronting George, but he knew the man would simply deny the whole conversation. Where, he would ask, was the proof? And why would he entrust the job of killing his wife to Takis and Mary when he could do it himself and make it look like an accident? An innocent smile would creep across his face as he feigned indignation to his fellow villagers.

If the village store was the place where men traded gossip, the women did their talking at the village spring. There, under the cool greenery, the women of Kupaki exchanged the latest rumors, their voices masked by the sound of water trickling into barrels, pails, and pots. Mary traveled to the spring and discretely extended the circle of people privy to the murderous machinations of George Nitsos, who, she fretted, planned to kill Panayota after he returned from his training—and then blame Takis and Mary.

Panayota caught wind of the rumor soon after it began to spread. Then she heard it directly from her cousin Thanasis, who approached her with the news one day beneath the shade of a scraggly old oak tree in the fields outside the village.

Thanasis, ever protective, was staring angrily at Panayota as he waited for a response.

"Don't look at me like that, Thanasis," she said. "You ask me why I didn't tell you. This is why. You look like you could kill now, and it doesn't make me feel better to know it's not me you want to kill but my husband. I don't want to be a widow any more than I want to be divorced. I still love George, you know. And I don't want you to go to jail for me by doing something stupid."

Thanasis's face softened. "I'm older now—and the father of four children. I'm not about to do anything insane and leave them orphans, much as I wish I could have it out with Nitsos. But I care about you. I want to protect you and do the best for your happiness and your safety. And frankly, I'm disappointed. I stood against half the village to get Nitsos to marry you. I threatened him when he seemed to be pulling out. Speaking of that, I don't remember you ever worrying about my temper back then. Now for your sake again, I'm asking you to leave that good-for-nothing criminal. I'd rather see you divorced than see you dead."

Panayota smiled ruefully. Part of her was angry at Thanasis for once again injecting himself in her affairs, but she knew he did so out of genuine love. He had always been protective of her. Likewise, she had for years nurtured an almost maternal feeling toward him, despite being eight years his junior. There was a child inside dear Thanasis, the gallant protector of women. Yet he had no clue about the inner life of women—or his own softer feelings. During his courtship of Polyxeni, Panayota had often scolded and advised him with all the freedom of an elder sister, and though he had always pretended to merely be humoring her, she knew by his actions that he had always valued her opinion and had taken her advice seriously. Now, though, she wondered if there was a way to soothe his anger while politely asking him to stand down.

"I know how much you love me, Thanasis—more than my brother, who has always loved me like it's his duty, and as much as my father, who I never got to know. And I'm grateful. But you know I grew up without my father's love because he went away to America to make a fortune for me to show his love for me, and your love for me is now demanding that I show I'm worthy of it by leaving my husband. Please don't make me do that."

"You don't seem to understand, Panayota. This isn't about me. This is about your life with someone who has already murdered you in his mind over and over again. And he will do it soon if you don't leave him now. He'll find someone with the guts he hasn't got to do it for him."

Panayota sighed. "You know George; he is like a child. He just says what he feels when he feels it. He is so loving when he has forgotten his anger, and now that girl has gone away from the village. Everything will be all right. I know it will be. So, let's stop being so gloomy."

"If you're going to continue pretending that nothing's wrong," Thanasis snapped, "I'll talk to that Linatsas myself!"

Panayota felt her heart quiver with fear. "Thanasis," she said, lowering her voice to a whisper, "don't." Unable to remain calm any longer, she could feel her eyes filling up with tears. "I beg of you. Please don't. Can't you see I'm doing everything to save my marriage? If it breaks up, there's nothing left for me to live for."

In all the years she had known him, Panayota had only cried in front of her cousin once—when he had resolved to force George to marry her. As she locked eyes with Thanasis, she could see that he, too, was fighting tears. Chastened, he turned and walked away.

See end of book for **Index of Names** of the people mentioned in this story. Also, on pages 68-72 there are useful **topographic photos**.

CHAPTER 8:
NO DEAL

MARY PAID A VISIT TO Alcapones at his hut, which was located across from Kupaki and halfway up St Nicholas Hill and found him alone.

Alcapones was a legend whose reputation extended well beyond the rugged village he called home. Barber. Lutist. Clarinet player. He was many things, but most knew him as a brilliant criminal who had committed countless audacious crimes over the years while somehow avoiding arrest. As someone who had outwitted the police and bribed judges, he was most infamous for an incident in the 1930s, when, commissioned by a girl's family to avenge a broken engagement, he carried out the act in the short time it took him to step outside and supposedly answer the call of nature during a concert. While his band continued to play, he disappeared, found his gun, and shot the erstwhile fiancé dead. He returned minutes later, the owner of a built-in alibi.

The fact that Mary had traveled to see someone as lethal as this man was a clear indication that Takis and Mary were running out of wiggle room. Since George Nitsos had returned from his stint with the army in mid-September, he had wasted no time in enlisting the couple in his plot to kill Panayota. He had already sent Mary on several missions to negotiate with potential killers, no doubt certain no one would ever suspect the woman of arranging a murder. Mary and her husband had managed to outmaneuver George by feeding him fictitious information or stretching out negotiations for weeks before feigning disappointment that a deal had fallen through.

When George had suggested she approach Alcapones, Mary had felt out of her depth. Now, standing just feet away from the legendary criminal, she felt her throat dry up with fear.

"What is it?" he asked brusquely.

"I'm here on behalf of George Nitsos," Mary said meekly.

Alcapones frowned, his eyes forming inscrutable slits. "Linatsas?"

"Yes," Mary answered nervously. "He has a proposal for you."

"Why doesn't he give it to me himself?"

"Oh, well," Mary stammered, "he's very busy."

"Linatsas?" the man looked skeptical. "What does the busy man want?"

"Well..." Mary couldn't bring herself to meet the old man's gaze, much less answer his question. "He's offering to pay you to ... kill his wife."

His eyes flashed something wild and white-hot. Surprise? Anger? Excitement? Mary wasn't sure. He was a cagey old one, impossible to read. He needed less than a second to recover himself and resume his steely countenance.

"How much?" he asked flatly.

Mary swallowed hard. She remembered her husband's words before her departure this morning: *Make it an offer that's easy to refuse.*

"Well," she said tentatively, "Mr. Nitsos has told me to tell you that the fee is negotiable. He—"

"Bah!" Alcapones replied, cutting her off with a wave of the hand. "Linatsas can do nothing for me." He turned his head slightly, eyeing Mary suspiciously. "And I want nothing from him. You tell him no deal." His eyes, icy until now, twinkled faintly. "Besides, in case you haven't noticed, I'm retired. I gave all that up a long time ago."

Mary felt her shoulders sag with relief. "Of course," she said in a voice barely above a whisper, the words catching in her throat. "I will tell him. Thank you. Good day."

After Alcapones refused the job, Mary told George that too many people knew about his plan, and it was time to stop before someone told the authorities. Had George pressed on that fall despite Mary's advice, he might have succeeded, given the civil war between Nationalists and Communists was raging all around the village and human life came to matter less than a flower by the side of the road at the mercy of any boy with a stick. Anyone caught in the wrong place at the wrong time might become the war's next victim.

George, with his con man's instincts, sensed that he couldn't run with the hare and hunt with the hounds forever. He and Panayota moved to Athens and thus removed himself from the daily tit-for-tat of the ongoing war. Living in the relative security of the capital was far safer than risking his life in our remote village. He returned only months later when the Nationalists, courtesy of the Marshall Plan, had gained the upper hand against the Communist guerillas. In fact, he was appointed as commander of his village militia, the aim of which was to assist the local police and tactical military Nationalists' units in their war against the guerillas.

Thirty men in the village, including Thanasis, were conscripted into George's unit and were armed with old rifles, plus hand grenades, land mines, and a machine gun mounted on a tripod. The machine gun was operated by Socrates. who was George's protégé and who the other men were calling the "small guy," with George being the "big guy."

Thanasis and Takis were nearly killed by the Communist guerillas on one occasion when George assigned them to patrol a hill near the village and failed to inform them, as they had agreed, when large forces of gorillas approached.

Not long afterward, and while the Communist guerillas were being pushed further away from the village, George and Panayota were hosting an evening dinner party at their home.

Panayota, having scurried about all day to make sure the home was impeccably tidied and decorated, was now busily looking after their guests. She didn't mind replenishing wine glasses, taking away dirtied dishes, or dressing the part of a beautiful hostess. In fact, she enjoyed entertaining guests and took pride in the reputation she had worked hard to gain as a first-rate cook and homemaker.

If anything nagged at her at all, it was the thought that George might do or say something to put everyone on edge. At the moment, he was standing in the living room with their guests and proudly showing off a gramophone he had recently bought. The story behind its purchase was one he loved to tell again and again.

"My love," he said, interrupting his tale long enough to address his wife, "bring us the wine from the table, would you?"

Panayota blushed. Most people in the village didn't believe in hanging their love for their spouses like banners for all to see. Such terms of endearment between married couples were reserved for private moments. Panayota knew, however, that while most of their dinner party guests would be embarrassed or shocked by the remark, others would find George's boldness charming. It was quite possible one or more of the ladies on hand would feel envious of such lavish talk.

She returned with a bottle of red wine, now half empty, and began topping off their guests' glasses.

"Thank you, darling," George said, eying her sweetly.

Again, her face flushed red.

The past several months had been a whirlwind, full of upheaval and conflict for Panayota. Between the war and their many moves, she oftentimes had felt literally out of breath. It felt good to be back in her village, amongst friends and family. True, many of the people they entertained were military officers and their wives just passing through the village, or government officials, also on their way to somewhere else.

"Bring me an ashtray," George said.

Panayota, who was talking to an officer's wife, didn't hear him until too late.

"Bring the ashtray and fuck your Christ!"

The room, bubbling with conversation just a second earlier, fell deathly silent.

Panayota felt the blood drain from her cheeks. She hurried to the kitchen and returned with an ashtray, smiling the whole time, hoping the others would see that her husband was just joking.

But George wasn't finished. "You whore," he spat, turning over the bottle of wine he had just drained. "Not even a fucking drop of wine in the bottle. How many times have I told you to take away bottles as soon as they're empty and put a full bottle on the table?"

"But we're not at the table," Panayota protested. "We're—"

"Just bring us more wine!" George snapped.

Panayota did as she was told, all the while wishing she could disappear. George was on a tear that night, and soon he was repeating the old joke about giving his wife away with a dowry if there were any takers. To her shame, all Panayota could do was joke along.

CHAPTER 9:
PARTNERS AND OPPOSITES

BY THE BEGINNING OF 1949, most of the Communist guerillas had been defeated, captured, or driven away, and all the villagers who had abandoned Kupaki for a safer environment had finally returned home. As a sense of normalcy returned to the village, new problems arose, problems that had nothing to do with fighting and everything to do with day-to-day living.

There was need for a leader, and George was ready to step into this role. Although some in the village, including Thanasis, thought of him as a bully who misused his authority, there were those who were impressed by his raw displays of power. None of the adults in our village seemed interested in challenging him. He had money. He had prestige. He had connections. If a government agent, policeman, military officer—anyone in a uniform—visited our village, he invariably went to George Nitsos first.

About the same time, the village's store owner had decided to sell his store, and Thanasis had spoken to him offering to take over the store himself. George was also making noises about reopening a store next door that years earlier had belonged to his uncle. A footpath no wider than four feet separated the two buildings front yards.

"Cousin," Panayota said one day after approaching Thanasis, "would you consider becoming business partners with my husband?"

Thanasis offered a look of disbelief. He didn't know whether to be incredulous, indignant, or both.

"Hear me out," Panayota said. "I know you have had your share of misgivings about George, but wouldn't it be better to have one large business together than two smaller businesses that must compete with each other? Why not become partners?"

Thanasis couldn't deny the logic in his cousin's argument. But going into business with a scoundrel like Linatsas struck him as foolhardy at best. George was irresponsible. Untrustworthy. Lazy. Would his reputation, not to mention the lamb-stealing story behind his nickname, undermine potential customers' trust? He would probably leave all the work to Thanasis, all the while provoking him into one needless argument after another.

No, Thanasis thought, the two men were far too different, and the list of reasons not to go into business with Linatsas was far too long. He opened his mouth to say no but hesitated when he saw the look on Panayota's face.

"You'll be less likely to argue if you're partners, rather than competitors," she said. "And I don't like it when you and George fight."

Her eyes, pleading and vulnerable, told Thanasis this had nothing to do with business. This was a cry for help. It was likely his cousin had convinced herself that she was merely suggesting a prudent consolidation of effort and resources, but in reality, she was asking for protection. With the war over, George had nothing to distract him from what had been his prewar obsession: the murder of his wife. Panayota, Thanasis suddenly realized, wanted to keep him close to the man who might kill her one day, to the husband she could never bring herself to leave.

Thanasis smiled gently at his cousin. She had always loved him like a brother, respected him like a father, and joked with and scolded him like a child. She trusted him instinctively— the same way she was now trying to pull him closer. It was doubtful she had thought too deeply about her reasons for suggesting he form a business partnership with her husband.

But he nevertheless felt compelled to honor her proposition. He thought back to his courtship of Polyxeni, to the days when he had let his loyalty to his family, particularly his father and his insistence on a handsome dowry, interfere with his love for Polyxeni. It was Panayota who had pulled him roughly into the light. Afterward, telling his father that Polyxeni was worth a thousand dowries had been the easiest thing in the world.

"All right," Thanasis said. "I'll consider it, Cousin."

In fact, as much as Thanasis distrusted George, he couldn't deny that there were good reasons for going into business with the man. George had worked at several large stores in Patras and thus had plenty of retail experience. He was a natural salesman—charming and persuasive. He certainly had the right contacts, not to mention a knack for making deals and striking bargains. And no one was more resourceful.

Suddenly Thanasis's misgivings seemed unimportant. Of course, it was one thing to talk himself into joining forces with George. It would be quite another to convince Polyxeni, his wife, that going into business with George Nitsos was a sound idea. Polyxeni knew nothing of the dangers Panayota was facing, and Thanasis, intent on protecting her, wanted to keep it that way.

When he presented the idea to Polyxeni, she offered a simple reply.

"As long as you remain only his business partner and do not become like him I can see nothing wrong with it. And as long as you come home the same husband I have known and the same father our children have known, all should be fine."

The store had only been open a few months before its owners clashed. The trouble began when a fresh round of American aid poured into our village, which, like the rest of Greece, was still benefiting from the Marshall Plan. George, the most connected man in Kupaki, was entrusted by government officials to oversee distribution, which would be based on the size and needs of each family. Some of the supplies were initially stocked at the old store George's uncle had owned, and some found their way to the store being run by George and Thanasis. Soon George was secretly hording the food and supplies and passing them out to his friends. When some villagers complained about receiving no part of the aid, George did not give an explanation but instead attacked and slapped several of them.

Thanasis then realized he'd made a grave mistake in opening a store with him. When he confronted George over the matter, an argument ensued, and a few days later George had transferred his share to his uncle's old store. Now the villagers were forced to choose between the two stores when shopping for supplies. Predictably, they split almost exclusively along family lines.

Panayota, though, refused to allow the division to remain. For three months, she went back and forth between the two men, trotting out the same arguments she had used on Thanasis before the partnership had begun. Once again, Thanasis gave in, and George moved his merchandise back to Thanasis's store. Thanasis and George were partners again.

As the partnership resumed, Thanasis managed the store's butcher shop while George managed the groceries—a proposal Panayota had made in order to keep the two men together yet separate under the same roof. Thanasis soon realized he was doing most of the work, but he didn't make an issue of it.

George, always more interested in partying and socializing than in working, also spent many days hunting. His most exclusive hunting partner and closest friend and protégé was Socrates Karaiskos. "The small one," as he had been known during the civil war, was in his mid-twenties. Taciturn, unemotional, cold, he was the opposite of his flamboyant ex-commander. Extraordinarily robust, he was George's strong arm. Thanasis often wondered if he was even human, or merely a machine. When he hunted for rabbits with George and the others, he was reputed to rarely miss his mark. After firing the lethal bullet, he would stand aloof and expressionless, his still-smoking gun in his hands, while the dogs sniffed wildly at the rabbit's still warm corpse.

As manager of the groceries and their inventory, George, instead of travelling to nearby towns, often proposed to go to Athens on the pretext of finding better prices.

True, the capital's bustling market offered more competition and lower prices, but Athens also happened to be where many of George's relatives lived. He could visit and stay with them and of course see his young friends who had recently moved there.

What Thanasis didn't know—and what would only come to light years later—was that after shopping at the market and spending time with his relations, George would then avail himself of what he had really traveled to Athens for: the wild life. Most of George's trips to Athens led to a night on the town. He would meet a handful of his old cronies, now policemen in Athens, at Omonoia Square downtown Athens and invite them to dinner at an expensive restaurant nearby, offering to pay for all those who seemed hesitant to go because of the cost. After several hours of feasting, drinking, and dancing at the restaurant, he would ask them to show him around their fair city. They would oblige, cringing in embarrassment as they carried the lurching and loudmouthed man, now unable to walk on his own powers.

Next, he would cajole them into taking him for a stroll through the red-light district. Some would assume it was curiosity leading him on. But those who had joined him in the past for one of his nights of debauchery would know better. Embarrassed to be seen amongst prostitutes and pimps, his uninitiated policemen friends would assume he merely wanted to ogle the women standing in the open doorways. After all, someone married to the likes of Panayota would never squander his time by spending it with prostitutes. But George would disappear inside, leaving his friends to pace outside while he finished his business. Then he would emerge, composing lurid, graphic verses about his just-completed conquest and singing them loudly in the street.

CHAPTER 10:
BEST FRIENDS

AFTER TUCKING US INTO BED one night, Polyxeni said goodnight to my siblings and me and then left for my parents' bedroom, where an oil lamp hanging from a wall peg cast a warm glow. Thanasis, as seemed to happen whenever George was out of town, was late. And Mother had a hunch she knew who he was with: Panayota.

Polyxeni slipped under the covers and then, after propping her head up on her elbow, reached with her free hand toward the lamp to lower the wick. A second later, the room was only dimly lit, with long shadows arcing across the floor.

Thanasis, she wondered, *what are you up to?*

As she stared up at the ceiling, her eyes slowly adjusting to the faded light, she tried to suppress the suspicion welling inside her. She knew well that one of the reasons she and Thanasis were husband and wife was because his cousin had lobbied so hard for him to her—and for her to him. And Panayota had been right: he had turned out to be a fine husband and father. Where was he now? Why had he missed supper?

When she heard the faint sound of the front door creaking open, she knew she would have an answer shortly. A moment later, Thanasis was lowering his body to the bed and emitting a tired sigh.

She rolled over to face him. "Where have you been?"

"I was at the Nitsos house—talking to Panayota."

Polyxeni briefly considered letting it go at that but then

thought better of it. "What is this, Thanasis? It seems you visit your cousin every evening when her husband is not home."

"I needed to talk to her."

"Always when George leaves? Is it something he cannot hear?"

Would he think she was jealous? Would he respond with evasiveness? She hadn't thought much about how he might react to her interrogation, but no amount of pondering could have prepared her for his reply.

"Listen, Polyxeni. George Nitsos has been trying to find someone to kill Panayota."

She gasped in disbelief. "What?"

"George has been planning this for years. He's actively looking for someone to do the deed."

Polyxeni still couldn't believe her ears. "Well, well," she said. "Is he going to slaughter her like a lamb? Who did Nitsos approach to do his dirty work for him?"

"A better question would be who he hasn't approached. He tried to hire Takis and Mary several years ago, and this month two more people came to me with stories of him trying to hire them to murder Panayota. He is promising them money or other rewards if they do it."

"But surely, Thanasis," she said, interrupting his list, "George Nitsos can't be that dumb. I can believe he's Godless enough to do that, but I never thought he was that stupid."

"But he's not stupid," Thanasis countered. "He's counting on people like you and me to assume he could never be so foolish as to ask an old woman like Mary or whoever else to murder his wife. That's all part of his plan. This is his clever mind at work. If anyone tries to confront him, he can easily deny the whole thing. Can't you see him now denying it? The fact that so many people are in on it can work in his favor. He can say the same thing as you, that it would be utterly foolish to plan such a thing and tell so many people. Who would believe such a thing?"

Polyxeni thought for a moment. She was still skeptical, but she could tell by the solemn look on Thanasis's face that he was worried. "And you say two more people approached you this month to tell you this?"

"Yes. That's why I went to see Panayota tonight after closing the store. I told her she must leave him, but she won't. She can't bear the thought of being the only divorced woman in Kupaki."

"These are just his empty threats to scare Panayota," Polyxeni said. She was determined to put Thanasis's mind at rest. "And empty threats they will remain. George Nitsos is like the air outside. Sometimes cool, sometimes hot. Sometimes strong, sometimes weak. Sometimes easterly, sometimes westerly. But never stable."

Having been reassured by his wife that George Nitsos was all talk, Thanasis began to concentrate more on his work and his family. He even joined George in another business venture, investing jointly in livestock Takis and Mary were looking after. Although teaming up with George made Thanasis queasy, he couldn't deny the social benefits. After all, George was one of the most important men in the village, what with his military rank, his part ownership of the store, and his marriage to Panayota, beloved by all. And of course, there was the money that kept arriving in envelopes from America, courtesy of George's father.

George, unfortunately, was all too aware of his influence in the village and grew increasingly arrogant as a result. He was especially intolerable toward women. He was good at earning money for the store—when he deigned to work, which occurred in spurts but just often enough for Thanasis to turn a blind eye to his excesses.

"George knows how to sell," Thanasis would say. The man used all the means at his disposal, including his contacts with influential people. If nothing else, Thanasis thought, keeping George close allowed him to continue to watch over and protect Panayota.

When George was elected village president, his ego grew even more bloated. "Because I am Nitsos," was the answer he gave many hapless people who dared question his judgment in municipal matters.

His arrogance extended to his horsemanship and to his horse, an excitable and unpredictable animal. Several young, athletic men, including Socrates, the strongest man in the village at the time and George's closest friend, had been unable to tame the animal. Soon after George took it for a brief successful ride, the horse broke into a gallop while he was on it, jumping and kicking for no apparent reason. George held on for a moment before he was thrown. He broke his leg in the fall and was forced to leave the village for a time to convalesce, only to return a few weeks later on a log stretcher.

Like many of the other children in the village, I was crestfallen after George's accident and throughout his absence. We children had hoped to witness the second coming of Alexander the Great, the great ruler who had once tamed the legendary wild horse, Bucephalus. But we had warm feelings toward George for other reasons, as well. He had just replaced Vas, whose authority as a village warden we hated, with his best friend Socrates Karaiskos.

Socrates, "the Small Guy" of the civil war, had recently bought a house near the center of the village and had married and started a family. At his wedding, he had chosen George, his mentor, as his best man. It was never explained how George had managed to give the village warden job to Socrates, who was barely literate, or how he had taken it away from Vas, a long-time adversary. Such appointments required a certain amount of paperwork and had to be approved by a dense bureaucracy. Was this a small coup?

All that anyone knew was that Socrates had ingratiated himself to George, enough to warrant a huge favor, and was by all accounts a member of the family. Even Panayota, the godmother of his baby girl, looked after him, showering him and his young wife with advice, money, and gifts.

Vas, meanwhile, had no choice but to accept his role as the odd man out. His relationship with George would only continue to break down.

In every village in Greece, lunch was always followed by a strictly observed siesta, especially in the hot summer, when the stifling afternoon heat was best avoided. In Kupaki, villagers would while away the time indoors, out of reach of the hot sun.

One day my older brother, didn't feel like resting. While the rest of the village napped, he and one of his friends loitered near the store, which was presently locked up and deserted.

My brother bored, kicked at a small stone. "There's nothing to do," he said forlornly. He didn't like how lonely the store felt. Normally, men smoked out front, or played cards, or absentmindedly fingered their worry beads, but right now those same men were wasting their lives in bed.

As if reading his mind, his friend pointed to several packs of cigarettes that were staring at them from inside the store. "We could smoke like the men," he offered.

"And play cards," my brother added.

The only thing preventing them from carrying on in place of the men was a set of iron bars covering the window.

Unable to get to the cigarettes and the cards, my brother decided to go home and get the key to the store. In no time, my brother and his friend were smoking and playing cards under a nearby tree when they were spooked by the sight of Socrates' dark face peering down at them. Socrates, who lived near the store, had seen everything.

Word then came from George that someone had stolen four hundred drachmas from the store's cash register. The two boys were beaten by their mothers but maintained their innocence about stealing the money. When Thanasis later returned from a trip, he spoke to Basil, who was an attorney, about the matter.

Basil was by nature a gentle and sophisticated man, a fatherly figure who looked after his orphaned nephew. He suggested the adults wait a day or two for the boys to succumb to the guilt that surely must be plaguing them, if indeed they had stolen the money. Thanasis agreed. Neither boy ever confessed to the crime. The truth, though, eventually came out when someone from the village came forward and admitted that George had given the store money that day to one of his cronies in the village.

Basil had been right. A guilty conscience had eventually produced the truth, but that conscience hadn't belonged to my brother or his friend.

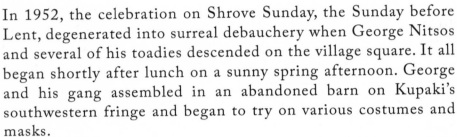

In 1952, the celebration on Shrove Sunday, the Sunday before Lent, degenerated into surreal debauchery when George Nitsos and several of his toadies descended on the village square. It all began shortly after lunch on a sunny spring afternoon. George and his gang assembled in an abandoned barn on Kupaki's southwestern fringe and began to try on various costumes and masks.

Dressed in two pairs of pants, one for its hind legs and the other for its forelegs, Socrates's donkey stood at the center of the mayhem. As the poor animal staggered along, several costumed men were taking turns riding it, although none lasted long before sliding off its back.

George led this motley group into the front yard of his next-door neighbor, and from there, with the help of the donkey's master, they advanced to the central square where all the villagers had assembled in reaction to all the commotion. As the group started line-dancing, the donkey, thoroughly spooked by now, suddenly emptied its bowels while simultaneously braying in alarm and was thus able to escape its tormentors, most of whom scattered, their hands covering their noses.

Just then, a diminutive female figure appeared. She was dressed in full police regalia. When it became clear she was scaring some of the young children, she removed her police cap, shook her hair free, and offered a reassuring smile. It was Panayota. Several villagers breathed a sigh of relief. Wasn't that just like her? Everyone knew Panayota was caring and sensitive and would never wish to frighten anyone, especially children.

Those of us watching had hardly exhaled when Panayota began to rip at her uniform and pull at her hair, digging her nails into her flesh and rocking back and forth. Was she possessed? Drunk? Only later would we learn that she had been driven to hysteria by George, who had argued with her violently that day, most likely even beating her, before leaving for his merrymaking.

Panayota, not normally so erratic, was by nature a gentle soul. It was obvious by the way she treated us Konandreas kids—showering us with hugs, kisses, and encouragement whenever she saw us—that she desperately wanted children of her own. Never mind the fact that George Nitsos behaved like a spoilt child himself, demanding all of her attention while insulting her and treating her cruelly. She even looked into adoption at one point, although unsuccessfully.

While Panayota acted like a tender mother toward the children of the village, George preferred the role of older brother. He clearly wanted to be our hero and was willing to do anything, including teaching us the facts of life long before we were ready to hear them, to win our adulation.

His behavior was at its worst when he was in the company of adolescent girls.

"You were born to make me suffer," he would call out to them as they passed the store, staring at their budding breasts.

Some of the men in the village, including Vas, the man whose job George as village warden had given to Socrates, warned him sternly to steer clear of their womenfolk. As the father of two pretty daughters in their late teens, Vas knew they were often the object of George's amorous advances.

When George crossed the line at a baptism in September of that year, it was Panayota who stepped in to save him.

Vas, having learned that George had positioned himself during the post-ceremony dance so that he could grab the girls' skirts as they passed by his chair, stormed through George's front door later that day.

"I could kill you today!" he shouted. He then nodded to

57

Panayota. "But I don't want to make this good woman a widow. Try your tricks with my girls again and I'll blow the brains clean out of that dirty head of yours!"

"Come on," George said, "it was just a joke."

George's reply only further enraged Vas, whose beet-red face looked ready to burst.

Panayota stepped in and managed to calm the indignant father with her soft words and charm. "My husband meant no harm," she said in a soothing voice. "He sometimes pushes too hard for a laugh, but his heart is in the right place."

Fortunately for George, most people in the village seemed to agree with Panayota's assessment. Good old George sometimes did or said things that were risqué, but he was harmless.

My parents were among the few who saw him for what he was.

"If I was your wife," Polyxeni once told him after hearing him hurl the usual vulgar abuse at Panayota, "we wouldn't have lasted an hour."

One night while my parents were cleaning up in the kitchen after dinner, my siblings and I were in our bedroom and doing everything we could to delay going to bed. We decided to play shop.

"Lesini is the watermelon!" my older brother announced, echoing George's famous sales cry. "Argos is the melon!"

"Herrings and sardines!" I retorted, not to be outdone.

We were talking loud enough for Thanasis to hear us, and I'm sure he was reacting to our playacting with some pride, although it's doubtful he appreciated the adoration in our voices as we mimicked his business partner.

But that pride certainly must have disappeared after my younger brother joined us in the concluding chorus. "Buy, fuck your Holy Virgin!"

Father rushed into our room, with Mother hot on his heels.

"What kind of language is this?" he demanded angrily.

My brothers and I cowered in the furthest corner of the bed, a heavy blanket pulled up to our chins. I was certain we were all about to be spanked, but relief followed when our father made it clear he simply wanted to establish why we had gotten it into our heads to say such an awful thing.

"Uncle Nitsos says that all the time," my older brother said.

"I know he does," Thanasis replied sternly, "but that doesn't mean you have to repeat it."

"But he's your partner!" I pointed out. "He does that at the store all the time."

"He's my partner, not my son," Thanasis retorted. "It's not my duty to bring him up properly. I know what to take from him and what not to. You don't. I have never repeated the filthy things he says. You did. So, I'm asking you now to stop imitating everything he says and does. And don't you ever repeat what you said."

Although I was confused, I nodded with the others. It didn't seem fair that adults could say things that children weren't allowed to repeat. One thing that was beginning to sink in, however, was that not everybody admired George the way we kids did.

CHAPTER 11:
NOBODY TO TALK TO

GEORGE NITSOS DIDN'T BOTHER TO hide his lecherous gaze. As the new schoolteacher studied, the damaged by time house of one of his friends, George let his eyes wander the graceful lines of her supple body.

The schoolteacher, young and unmarried, had arrived a few weeks earlier just in time for the new school year. Some said she was too young and had only a few months of teaching experience. Others said she had a way with the children that encouraged them to work harder. All George cared about was that she was easy on the eyes—fresh meat, as it were, for a man whose appetites were not easily satisfied. He had arranged for her to stay at the house across the street from his house.

A few weeks after her arrival, she had been appointed to a local committee whose duties included examining buildings that had been burned down during the German and Italian occupations and the civil war. At the moment, she was viewing what was left of a house that belonged to one of George's friends. Her report would help determine how much, if any, government aid would be granted to help fund renovation.

George felt his patience ebb; he knew his flattery was having little impact on the teacher. Indeed, she had a serious, no-nonsense air about her that grated on him. She appeared impervious to his charms. Most girls blushed when he flirted with them, but she kept him at arm's length. She had to be aware of her own attractiveness, her fresh good looks, her youthful allure. She positively oozed sensuality. And yet here she was going about her business as if her only intention was to appraise this building. Her aloofness was maddening.

George, impatiently shifting his weight from one foot to the other, glanced away at the surrounding hillsides, which would soon begin to show fall color.

The village vacationers had already completed their mass exodus for the heated apartments and schools of crowded Athens. The swallows, too, had abandoned their mud nests so carefully constructed in balconies all over the village and migrated south, toward the warm shores of North Africa. With flocks flying overhead, Kupaki's shepherds had left the open hilltops around the village and made for the lowlands and their sheep cots and manger-like enclosures. Fall was an exciting time of transition, George thought, a sensual feast of riotous colors and bold scents. But it was lost on this dour schoolteacher.

Finally, the schoolteacher was ready to offer her assessment. "I'm sorry this man's house is in such bad condition, Mr. Nitsos," she said. "But I cannot attest that the damage has been caused by fire. I see no evidence of that."

George unfolded one of his patented smiles. "I can assure you this place was burnt down during the occupation," he said, unleashing all his charm. "I've seen many such buildings during my time as commander."

"And I have lived all my life in a village," the fetching young schoolteacher responded. "My house is built with the same materials as this one. I know how burnt wood and stone look, and it's definitely not like this."

George felt his jaw drop. His charisma was obviously wasted on this pathetic excuse for a woman.

"I'll hang up your bread, you bitch!" he shouted, referring to the way villagers hung their loaves from trees to prevent foxes and other scavenging animals from eating them.

Fortunately for our new schoolteacher, George spent most of the winter in nearby towns. As our village's council president, he sat in on several meetings dedicated to the construction of a new road connecting Kupaki with several area villages. In fact, nobody thought much about his frequent absences. Only later would we learn that between these meetings there were a few romantic ones, as well.

On May Day 1953, true to Greek tradition, our village celebrated with a grand picnic atop a small peak that rose just southwest of the village. To usher in the spectacular spring day, the schoolteacher led us schoolchildren in a fitting opening ceremony with a song about flowers and wreaths she had been teaching us for days.

The villagers lined the saddles of their horses with multicolored homespun blankets and loaded the animals with satchels bulging with picnic food and wicker-cradled demijohns filled with ouzo and local red wine for the half-hour trek.

After reaching the summit, we took in the glorious view, which encompassed several nearby villages, plus a river below and some of its tributaries. Soon spits were erected by the more energetic of the adults, while others, mostly the older among them, happily spread blankets on the ground nearby and flopped down to rest. Later that afternoon, after the meal, the villagers, aided by red wine, danced the traditional line Greek dances, with Thanasis and Panayota leading the revelry.

While everybody was mixing it up with everybody, dancing and exchanging wishes, George was exclusively in the company of the local police captain. They did not dance but instead murmured to each other whenever a pretty young maiden led the dance. The villagers knew George and the captain were good friends, often visiting each other during the past few months, but it was always thought the ex-captain and the new were just bodies joined by the fate of authority.

By the time the dancing finally came to an end, many of the men were so drunk they were betting on who could roll downhill the farthest. While cheered by everyone, Thanasis, his face flushed, kept singing and dancing but his steps were no longer surefooted. I could see Polyxeni was not pleased with his condition. She had bruised her shin after falling from her horse during the ride to the summit and thus had been watching the dancing instead of participating. She laughed at Father's behavior at first, but now I could tell she was ready to put her foot down.

"Thanasis," she said firmly, "that's enough. You'll get sick. Time to go home."

When some other men's wives also intervened by asking their husbands to stop, the men, including Thanasis, pretended—and declared with much hand-gesturing—that they had no knowledge who the women were and that they had never met them in their lives. The situation further aggravated Polyxeni.

Panayota stepped in, saying, "Let the men have fun, Polyxeni dear." She was giggling like a schoolgirl. "They're doing fine. It's only a little wine."

Her words, unfortunately, did nothing to appease Polyxeni, who told her as much.

Panayota, giggling a second earlier, stopped abruptly, the mirth in her eyes disappearing like the flame of a snuffed-out candle. "You should have someone else, Polyxeni," she said, her eyes moving to stare at George, "to tell you every day, 'Fuck your virgin and your God.' Then you would know!"

Her words had a humbling effect on Polyxeni, as they did on me.

Father, though, appeared ready to go home. As he staggered off in the vague direction of our village, still mumbling the lyrics to the song, I knew he had just enough presence of mind to find his way home.

The festivals continued into summer, and on the day of the annual village's festivity, in late July, everybody gathered in the village square to eat, socialize, and dance.

Central square dancing. Alekos Tsipras, the teacher of philosophy, is holding a young village maiden, who leads. At the top of the photo, spectators have gathered in the front yard of the store belonging to George and Thanasis. The bottom of the photo is near the spot where Panayota read George's love letter to Poly.

As usual, George and Thanasis had a bird's-eye view of the celebration from their store, which overlooked the square. But when the dancing started at 6:30 pm that evening, it would have been better had George not been able to see Poly, his erstwhile love interest, who had returned from Athens to partake in the festivities. Now in her mid-twenties, Poly was a striking beauty, and she made a lovely dancing partner for the older brother of my mother and her cousin, a handsome air force man with startling blue eyes and an athletic build. Dressed in his immaculately clean and pressed white uniform, he took hold of Poly's kerchief and joined her as they led the circular Greek dance at the exact spot where Panayota had stood and read aloud the letter sent by George to her some years ago.

All eyes seemed to follow the couple putting on a brilliant display of grace and beauty. Furtively, one by one, the villagers began to shift their gaze from the attractive couple to the man who had once besieged her and had scandalously vied for her affections until her father had been forced to take her away. They wanted to see how George would react to the sight of

Poly's lips, which were parted like a half-opened rose, as she smiled to her cousin, now holding her. How would her former illicit suitor respond as she spun gracefully in another man's hands just a few yards away?

The display appeared to set George on fire. He took a drag from his cigarette, inhaling deeply, and then jerked his gaze away from the dashing couple and stared down at the slate tiles beneath his feet.

After that night, George rarely played cards at the store. His jokes grew less profane, and he could be seen spending more time in lonely contemplation on a bench at the store.

Panayota, meanwhile, seemed happier than she had been for some time.

"Our prayers are answered," Polyxeni told Thanasis one night. "Thanks to the Holy Virgin, there is peace again under Panayota's and George's roof. Long may it last."

Panayota was always so cheerful and ladylike; hearing George utter blasphemous vulgarities against her had shocked Polyxeni to the core. Polyxeni had no idea what it was like to be mistreated by a husband, to live in a world of abuse and fear.

Now, though, it appeared things were finally improving between the couple, but Polyxeni's euphoria didn't last long.

Just days later, her sister-in-law Papadia, Papazois's wife, relayed to her an early-morning encounter she'd had with Panayota.

"I found Panayota sleeping in a barn just on the outskirts of the village," Papadia told Polyxeni. "She tried to deny it at first, but then she cried and admitted things aren't going well with George. I told her she should divorce the man, but she refuses. She doesn't want to be the subject of village gossip. She doesn't want to be Panayota Soulias again."

The fact that Panayota was spending nights sleeping outside her house made Polyxeni agonize over her safety. Had Thanasis been wise to take George's machinations seriously?

—————————— ✒ ——————————

Toward the end of August 1953, Panayota was watering the beans in her garden near the village spring, when Marula, whose house butted up against the garden, approached her.

"How is the crop, Panayota?" Marula asked as she entered the garden.

"Hello, Marula. The crop is fine."

Marula, like Panayota, was a slender woman who stood less than five feet tall. The bean plants, supported by cedar stakes, towered over her, forming a maze of arches overhead. The sound of trickling water could be heard from the nearest ditch, not to mention the irrigation pool nearby, although it was nearly drowned out by the buzzing of bees pollinating the bean flowers overhead.

"Panayota," Marula said in a soft voice, "I have something I need to tell you."

Panayota straightened. "What is it?"

"Effie saw your husband kissing Katina outside the store and then again inside. She was so shocked to see a married man kissing a young woman that she didn't know what to do. She is a very ethical girl and finally came to me at the village spring and confessed what she saw. She asked me not to tell anyone because she is afraid of George, but I knew I must tell you. You have a right to know."

Panayota felt the blood drain from her face. Effie was Marula's goddaughter. She was young, but trustworthy. If she said it was true, then it was likely true. As for Katina, she was a pretty young brunette who carried herself with a poise that made her look older than what she really was: eighteen. What had George gone and done? Panayota wanted to deny the story, to say there must be some kind of mistake. But she knew there was no point.

"Did anyone else see this?" she finally asked.

"No. Only my Effie."

"And she has told no one else?"

"No one."

Her secret, Panayota knew, wouldn't stay that way for long, not in Kupaki. "Oh, dear Marula!" she lamented. "I have great, great many troubles, and I have nobody to talk to!"

"You have nobody to talk to?" Marula countered. "You have cousins and cousins here, and you have a brother and sister you can write, and you tell me you have nobody to talk to? Go and talk to them, you. Go and talk to them. What are you waiting for?"

Panayota did have several blood relations in the village, but she spoke to only one person about George's secret: Effie. She met her on a village path one day and told her that the gossip she was spreading about her husband was damaging his reputation in the village. Effie, clearly embarrassed, pretended she knew nothing and had spoken to nobody. It was obvious she was afraid of George.

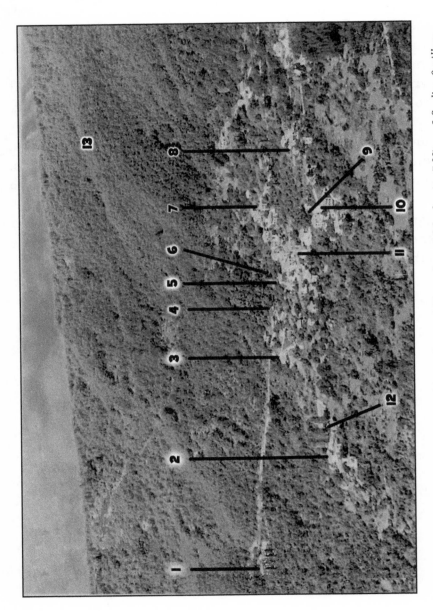

1.Cemetery; 2.Church St.George; 3.Zakkas; 4.Gumas; 5.Konandreas; 6.Murder site; 7.Nitsos; 8.Soulias; 9.village spring;10.Neighbors house where Panayota worked; 11.Central square; 12.School; 13.Oak tree covered summit.

BETTER DEAD THAN DIVORCED

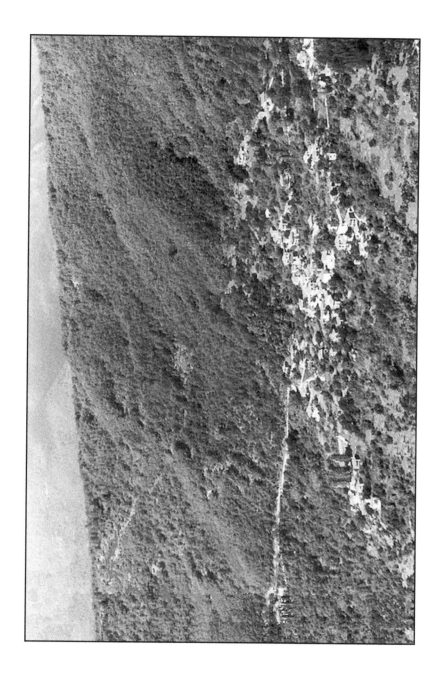

LUKAS KONANDREAS M.D.

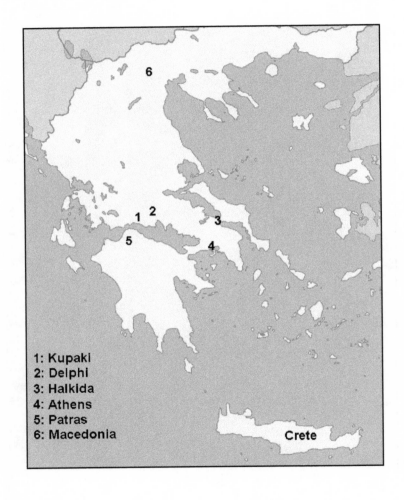

1: Kupaki
2: Delphi
3: Halkida
4: Athens
5: Patras
6: Macedonia

Crete

70

1. Church of St. George 2. School 3. Zakkas 4. Hill hiding the Goumas House 5. Konandreas 6. Nitsos 7. Soulias 8. Central Square 9. House of youth's party

*1. Zakkas 2. Gumas 3. Konandreas 4. Nitsos 5/6. Central square and youth's party house 7. Oak trees covered hill over village * Murder site + Gumas Yard*

PART II

CHAPTER 12:
CRACKS IN THE FAÇADE

ON SUNDAY, SEPTEMBER 6, 1953, I watched from the altar of St. George Church as my fellow villagers, responding to the invitation of the bells pealing overhead, began to arrive for the morning service. The spiritual hub of our small village, St. George was so old that no one, not even the oldest men with ancient shepherds' crooks in their gnarled old hands, had seen the raising of its walls, now cracked.

Kupaki's St. George Church in 1951. The walls, still cracked, had yet to undergo renovation. Papazois, the priest, stands at the entrance.

At eight years old, I had been made an altar boy by Papazois, the village priest. Papazois, wore a gold-colored robe and a long, flowing white beard. The smell of stone, wood, and incense filled me with a sense of contentment, as did the sight of everyone dressed in their Sunday best. As the villagers entered, their shoes making muffled sounds on the stone, they brought with them wafts of newly laundered clothes and fresh tobacco. I counted them idly, eventually topping out at about one hundred and twenty people, half of which were visitors who would be leaving when the weather turned cold.

The men, taking their customary place, assembled to the right of the center aisle, while the women gathered to the left. Several church council members sat behind the counter near the back of the nave, including Thanasis, who was the vice president, and George Nitsos, the president.

"With fear of God," Papazois proclaimed, his voice softened by his long white beard, "faith and love, draw near."

As he chanted, he lifted with both hands the holy chalice, which was covered with a scarlet veil.

Most parishioners moved forward to receive Communion, but George left the counter, took a couple steps toward Papazois, and then, as if remembering something, changed course toward the doors.

"Receive me today, oh Son of God," Papazois said, "as a partaker of the Mystic Feast."

One by one the pious made the sign of the cross and approached the priest. With the scarlet veil under their chins, they opened their mouths to receive the bread and the wine, the flesh and the blood of the Savior.

"For the deliverance of sins and for eternal life..."

Once outside, George walked across the churchyard toward a huge mulberry tree beside the compound's low stone wall. Shaded from the sun by the tree's enormous canopy, he sat down on the wall and faced the church. From the thick shade he studied the spectacular panorama of rolling hills and mountain peaks that opened up in every direction. He fumbled in his pockets and, after fishing a cigarette free, lit it and drew the smoke into his lungs hungrily.

He didn't notice Katina, who had exited her house next to the church compound, until she was walking confidently toward him.

"Just came to say hello," the pretty young brunette said after he gave her a questioning look.

"Hello."

"Do you want me to bring you a chair?" she asked.

George didn't answer, and instead waved her away. At the end of the service, little groups of people started to form outside the church. Several of the men huddled near the front entrance of the church, where they discussed the state of the building. As they leaned backward and tilted their heads upward, they pointed to the big cracks in the stone walls that extended from the foundation to the roof. George, to the surprise of many present, lingered beneath the great old mulberry tree nearby, seemingly uninterested. As the president of the church council, he normally jumped at the chance to join such a discussion, but today he was uncharacteristically aloof.

After a few minutes, the villagers slowly began to disperse. Most took the main cobblestone path that climbed sharply uphill toward the village center. The women and children would continue homeward, while the men would gather in front of George and Thanasis's store.

The summer visitors, mostly former locals now living in Athens, would play cards; talk passionately about politics, hunting, sex, and old feuds; and encourage the elderly among them to spin their yarns about the good old days. The locals, in turn, would want the Athenians to describe all the details of life in the big city—its modern, eccentric customs, the loose women, the amazing spectacles they'd read about in the newspapers.

The discussions would last until one o'clock in the afternoon, at which time they would leave the store and head home for lunch and their customary siesta, eventually lulled to sleep by the drone of cicadas.

After the siesta, Thanasis was the first to return to the store that Sunday afternoon but soon the village men started to arrive. I spent the afternoon on the move. There were games to be played, and a modest amount of work to be done. The latter included fetching fresh spring water for home and for Thanasis's customers at the store, taking our horse to the spring to drink, and completing small chores around the house for Polyxeni and grandmother, as well as next door for my great-uncle and great-aunt. As was so often the case, I migrated between the store, the village square, and home, never staying anywhere for too long.

By about 6 pm that evening, the oak-covered summit over the village had begun to cast its long shadow over the village. I watched from our house as the last swarms of bees hurried to their hives in the dappled sunlight. The day, like most in September, had been warm and dry, with temperatures peaking at ninety degrees and everyone in the village scurrying to the shade. Now, with the sun receding, the air was pleasant and mild, though still lacking the slightest trace of humidity. It seemed funny to me that just as the bees were scurrying home, the villagers were beginning to emerge from their houses.

While the children played soccer and hide and seek, some of the grown-ups were watering vegetable gardens from water collection pools made from clay. Others were taking their goats to graze on the low rolling hills surrounding the village. And the young adults were looking for a gramophone for a party for the community youth, given at the house of a man near the village square.

A few houses away, Panayota had just stopped in to visit Aggelo, her cousin. After the two women shared tidbits of gossip and spoon sweets—sweetened fruit preserves served on a spoon—Panayota left for the Zakkases' house, where she joined her sisters-in-law and several other women.

They sat on the front verandah, chatting and watching dusk change the color of the peaks from gold to amber, then purple.

It was a familiar-yet-spectacular sight that still gave Panayota goose bumps. While the sun traveled west, the shadow of the summit over the village covered the upper half of the village first, then the church and the school. Once the shadow had advanced further down to the brook, it would creep up the other side, ascending the hill of St. Nicholas like water filling one of the buckets at the village spring. Panayota, like other locals, had seen the ascent of the shadow on the oak covered summit over the village so often she could tell time by it—and know how many minutes of daylight remained.

Soon the temperature would fall to roughly sixty degrees, where it would stay for the remainder of the night. Panayota wrapped her arms around her shoulders, anticipating the moment later tonight when, after she had retired to bed, she would pull a blanket up around her neck.

By 8 pm, I had finished playing games and doing my chores and was eating dinner with my brothers and sister and Grandma Mia on our covered veranda, which looked out toward the west, now only faintly glowing from the last vestiges of the setting sun. Mother was there. So, too, Aunt Aggelo, who had dropped by for a chat. Father was still working at the store and as usual wouldn't return until much later after my siblings and I had gone to bed, at which time he and Polyxeni would eat their dinner.

While the grownups talked, night was rapidly falling. Fireflies danced just beyond the light cast from a small oil lamp hanging from a peg on the wall, and somewhere out there in the darkness the many-toned jangling bells of the goats that were being herded back to the village from the hills could be heard, along with a chorus of crickets chirping in the dry grass and frogs croaking from the irrigation pools.

At about half-past eight, Panayota called to us from a pathway that passed above our house. *"Kale orexe!"* she said. *"Bon appétit!"*

She was walking with one of her husband's cousins.

"Come in and have some dinner with us!" Polyxeni called back.

"Thanks," Panayota replied, "but it's getting late. I'd better go. *Kalinikta*. Goodnight." By the time she got home, the night was pitch black. No moon hung in the sky.

She'd hardly stepped inside, when she heard a sound outside. One of George's shepherds had stopped at her door on the way to his hut to borrow a flashlight.

Around 9 pm, Panayota gazed out the window at the lights beginning to appear on the distant hills, where the shepherds were lighting fires, the flames raging high for a few minutes and then subsiding into smaller flickers of yellow. She had lived in Kupaki long enough to know that mothers all over the village were hustling still-awake children to bed.

"Panayota! Panayota!"

A faint echo from several houses away grew in volume when one of Panayota's neighbors took up the call.

"What is it?" Panayota asked from her doorstep.

"It is George's sister and they want you to go to the Zakkases," the neighbor answered.

"But I just came from there."

"They say George is staying for dinner. They are asking you to join them."

Panayota shook her head in dismay before trudging over to the neighbor's house, so she could communicate directly with her sister-in-law.

"I've just come from there!" she hollered. "I've changed into my house robe and haven't got a flashlight!"

The other woman took a few moments to relay the message to her brother. "George says come as you are for a little while! It's only us, anyway! Come and have some dinner and some company!"

"I'm afraid to come by myself without a light!" Panayota replied.

Once again there was a pause while the message was relayed to George.

"Panayota, George is going to come a little way up by the brook and bring you back so you won't be alone for the darkest part!"

"Allright!"

Panayota gingerly descended the cobblestone path that passed above our house. There was still no moon, although the stars were bright, as were the fireflies flitting nearby and the shepherd's fires burning on the distant hills. When she reached the two brooks under the big maple trees, she was enveloped in utter darkness. She could hear music and laughter coming from the party for the village youth, just a few houses away.

CHAPTER 13:
DRUMS AND GUNS

PANAYOTA WAS RELIEVED TO SEE George's slim silhouette up ahead on the path, where he was waiting for her. He offered his arm, and she gladly accepted it as they walked the darkest stretch of the path, with George pausing every so often to strike a match to illuminate their way. It was at times like this, when George flouted tradition and made his affection for her public, albeit in the darkness, that Panayota appreciated her husband's boldness.

This is his true self, she thought. *If only he could temper his impulses and behave like a gentleman all the time.*

They reached the Zakkas home and sat down for dinner, followed by a smoke. Soon a card game was underway at the dining table.

"Aren't you going to play?" George asked.

"Not tonight," Panayota said and curled up on an armchair nearby. Normally she enjoyed playing cards, but tonight her eyes felt heavy and sleep beckoned.

She drifted off to the noises coming from the party the village youth were having a few houses away. It sounded like a raucous gathering of young people, with dancing, music and plenty of shouting. Panayota could still remember what the village had been like before Nick's dance lessons during the occupation. The older generation had resisted initially, but now dancing was no longer a stolen pleasure but a fashion statement. The tango, the waltz, the fox trot—the young people could do it all. Between outbursts of laughter and cheering, Panayota heard the recorded voices of several popular Greek singers. No doubt the partygoers, already light-headed with wine and ouzo, were snatching lukumi, a gelatinous square-shaped sweet similar to Turkish Delight, from platters as they rested between songs.

George and the others played a couple of rounds of cards before Panayota roused herself on the armchair. Feeling foggy and uncomfortable, she caught her husband's attention at the table.

"I'm not feeling very well, George," she complained. "Can we go home?"

"George," one of her sisters-in-law said, "you'd better take her home."

"Yes," another chimed in, "she looks really pale."

"In a little while," George said, glancing down at his watch. "Let me just finish this one."

Only a few minutes earlier, the men playing cards and trading stories at the store had finished for the night, and after they left, Thanasis closed up shop. Accompanied by one of his brother-in-law, an Athenian policeman who was vacationing at the village, Thanasis walked slowly up the path toward home. He could hear music being played on a gramophone and echoing from the party next door.

"Would you like to eat dinner with us?" the policeman asked.

"I would," Thanasis said. He made a quick stop home to let Polyxeni know where he was going and then continued on to the Gumas residence, where he ate dinner with his in-laws.

"Do you need a light?" his mother in-law asked after he'd had his fill and was ready to go home.

"No," Thanasis answered, "I'll be all right. The starlight is enough for me to see by."

He walked home and found his mother asleep, along with his four children. Polyxeni, meanwhile, had fallen asleep outside on the balcony, no doubt savoring one of the last remaining mild nights of the summer.

"Come to bed, Polyxeni," he said, gently shaking her.

When she didn't respond, he thought better of disturbing her and decided to let her sleep on the balcony. A few moments later, he was lowering his head onto his pillow. Exhausted after a long day's work, he quickly fell asleep.

On any other night, the village would have been quiet by now, save for the crickets chirping and the occasional hoot from an owl or howl from a jackal, barely audible in the distance. Tonight, though, as the clock struck eleven, the youth at their party had switched from what they called "European dancing" to traditional Greek line dancing and the party was still in full swing.

At the Zakkas gathering, meanwhile, and much to Panayota's relief, George appeared finally ready to say goodbye. Their hosts gave them a flashlight, and soon they were walking sharply uphill along the curved path that led toward their home, Panayota walked in front, followed by George with the flashlight.

On this starlit September evening, all of Kupaki reverberated to the racy dance number now blaring from the youth's party gramophone.

The drums they thump!
Thump went a drum.
The drums they boom!
Boom went a deeper drum.

The song, more famous for its rhythm than for its lyrics, now wove the two together.

The drums they thump and boom and boom and thump and boom!

At the party, a young maiden dazzled onlooker as she led the energetic Greek dance called the Syrto. Moving in time to the beat, she twisted and turned; leapt effortlessly, her skirt swirling grandly; and then landed lightly on her feet with feline grace.

Thump and boom and boom and thump and—

Boom!

Everyone heard it. Was it part of the music? Some stopped dancing.

Then it came again, this time out of time with the music. *Boom!*

The dancers froze. They'd all heard it this time. Someone switched off the gramophone.

"That wasn't a drum!" one of the women said worriedly.

The percussive blast had come from the darkness outside. The partygoers stood still, straining their ears as echoes bounced off the surrounding hills.

"It's a gun!" several said in unison.

The dogs in the neighborhood, smelling fear, suddenly began to howl.

"It was near the ravine!"

"Who can it be?"

"It wasn't from the party, was it?"

I must have been asleep for about half an hour when the music I had dozed off to ceased suddenly, replaced by the menacing peal of gunshots, followed by a jumbled chorus of howling dogs, crying babies, and shouting neighbors. I could hardly move in the bed from the fearful, almost choking, embrace of my younger brother.

"What's happening?" he cried.

"I don't know."

"Mama! Baba!" I called, unable to calm my quavering voice. "What's going on?"

My parents didn't answer, although I could hear them hurriedly dressing in their room.

"The bastard has killed her," Thanasis muttered angrily before rushing outside with Polyxeni.

Who? I wondered fearfully. Who is the bastard? And who has he killed?

My mind raced as I tried to piece together what little I knew.

I felt confident my immediate family was safe—my father and mother, my brothers and sister, my grandmother—but that was all I could be sure of.

My brother and I, too afraid to leave the safety of our old, dilapidated bed, were soon joined by our older brother, who had also been calling to our parents. Now we gathered in the darkness. We sank deeper into the bed, and soon we were covered by the blanket. It was too dark to see my brothers, but I could feel the bed trembling with our collective fear. We huddled together, teeth clenched, knees tucked beneath our chins. Normally we fought to stay clear of the dip in the middle, itself a casualty of too many days and nights spent jumping and tumbling on the ancient bed. It was always the most uncomfortable place to sleep, and we typically went to great lengths to claw our way from its sweaty clutches, preferring the side closest to the balcony and the cool night air and starry sky. Tonight, we huddled together in its hot, protective sag.

I tried to open my eyes, hoping to stir up enough courage to face the frightening commotion just outside our window. It was no use. My imagination ran wild as I conjured up all kinds of horrors unfolding out in the darkness.

From the direction of the Gumas house, about a hundred yards away, a woman was calling out to a neighbor, a dentist who lived in the middle of the village. Someone was injured badly, she was saying, and was in desperate need of a shot of Aramine.

My brothers and I inched toward the balcony, but no one wanted to be the first to cross the threshold. Instead, we recoiled in fear. Several times we made our way toward the balcony, and several times fear stopped us in our tracks. It was a deep, primeval fear, a fear I felt in the pit of my stomach, a fear I had never known.

Finally, the youngest of the three of us, was the first to venture out onto the balcony, and we followed. We stepped out into a moonless night and stared down at the vineyards below, where shadows were scurrying in every direction. People shouted. Horses neighed. Lanterns swung. Our village looked like a fairground at night, but danger, not festive joy, hung in the air. The pungent aroma of horse dung filled my nostrils, followed by wafts of peroxide and kerosene. Fireflies shone brightly like stars. The surrounding hills, which had earlier glowed with small fires lit by the shepherds keeping watch, were now swathed in darkness.

"Mama! Baba!" my brothers and I shouted, making communication from the Gumas house impossible. *"Mama! Baba!"* we shouted again.

There was no response.

We ran back to our sagging bed and crawled under the covers once again.

CHAPTER 14:
"YOU HAVE DEVOURED ME"

AMID A TANGLE OF DISTRAUGHT and disoriented voices saying, "The Nitsoses! Someone murdered the Nitsoses," my parents were the first to arrive at the Gumas yard, where Gumas the policeman had gently lowered and propped up a screaming Panayota against a stone wall. The light from a kerosene lantern exposed blood flowing in rivulets from between Panayota's legs downhill toward the middle of the yard. She appeared to have been shot in the chest or abdomen—Thanasis couldn't quite tell.

Very soon the partygoers from the youth's party and other villagers coming from their houses were hurriedly arriving.

George, who was able to walk, had just been helped into the yard and was staring at the gathering crowd with dazed eyes. "They have killed us tonight!" he said, repeating the phrase several times.

In fact, aside from a few superficial wounds, George looked to Thanasis to be largely unscathed. Two tiny rips in his pants showed near his left knee, plus another a few inches lower, as if he had walked through one of the thorny thickets nearby. There was no blood to speak of, and he was able to walk freely.

"Panayota!" Polyxeni rushed to Panayota's side and began cradling her head, which was lolling from side to side.

"Oh, Polyxeni," Panayota moaned, her voice growing hoarse, "They've killed me! They've killed me!"

"How did this happen? Who did this to her?" Polyxeni looked around wildly at the villagers gathering in the yard.

Thanasis, overwhelmed by rage and despair, clenched his fists repeatedly as he stood next to Polyxeni.

Panayota stared up at him with pleading eyes. "Thanasis," she said, weeping in pain, "They have killed me. Do you think Vas has killed me?"

Vas, the man whose job George had handed to Socrates, the man whose teenage daughters George had coveted, certainly had reason to hate George Nitsos, but Thanasis knew he wasn't responsible for tonight's shooting.

"No!" he snapped. "It wasn't Vas! I told you who would kill you!"

He was furious. Furious at his cousin for ignoring his warnings. Furious at himself for not doing more to protect her. Furious at the man he knew was behind this. Thanasis could hardly look at George, whose mere presence filled him with bitterness.

George's sisters, now crouched beside Panayota, were trying to make her more comfortable by rubbing her arms and placing pillows beneath her head.

"A doctor!" someone shouted. "Get a doctor!"

The words galvanized Thanasis into action, and soon he was barking orders like an army captain. Horses were saddled. Men were dispatched to summon the doctor and the police.

"Mama. Mama." Panayota's voice was feeble now.

"Someone get Skevi, Panayota's mother," said a teacher of philosophy vacationing at the village. "And Papazois."

The teacher had just uttered aloud what Thanasis—and likely everyone else standing in the Gumases' yard—was thinking. Expert medical help at such short notice was all but unavailable in remote Kupaki. Although the others were fighting to keep her alive, Thanasis knew Panayota was dying. Peroxide and hastily assembled bandages were a poor substitute for life-saving care.

A priest, on the other hand, was readily available. Summoning Papazois to administer Holy Communion was not only the prudent thing to do, but also their solemn duty as good Christians.

George, meanwhile, walked inside and asked Aliki Gumas, the householder, to make him coffee. "And make it real coffee," he said. "I don't drink coffee with chicory."

He then returned to the courtyard and knelt beside his wife. "Panayota, oh my Panayota," he murmured. "Why you? Why you?"

One of his cousins was rubbing his leg, where the two small rips in his pants were visible.

"Rub him," Thanasis muttered as he paced past George. "That's right. Rub him. A rubbing is what he needs now."

What he really needed, Thanasis thought, was a bullet. Immersed in increasingly dark thoughts, Thanasis barely heard Basil when he approached him.

"Thanasis," Basil said, "we need to phone the doctor in Krokylion."

The only telephone in Kupaki was in the village store. Basil, the kind attorney who had urged patience after my older brother and his friend had been accused of stealing money from the store, was once again offering wise counsel.

"Come with me," the attorney said. "Let's go quickly."

Thanasis followed him from the courtyard and into the darkness. But after only walking a few feet, he stopped dead in his tracks. It was too late for a doctor—he knew that. But it wasn't too late to punish George for what he had done.

"What's the matter?" Basil asked.

"He killed her," Thanasis said through gritted teeth.

"Who killed whom? Who are you talking about?"

"Him," Thanasis answered. "Linatsas. He killed her."

"You mean George killed Panayota?" Basil appeared dumbstruck. "Thanasis, Panayota is still alive, and she might not die if we get on with it and get the doctor here. You're upset. You're forgetting that George was shot, too."

"Exactly," Thanasis said. "He killed her. The scheming bastard got someone to kill Panayota."

"Do you realize what you're saying?"

"I'm going to get my gun and blow his brains out."

"Look here, Thanasis," Basil said, adopting the tone of a cautious lawyer, "if what you're saying is right, it's a matter for the police. Leave it to them."

"He's been trying to get her killed for ages. I know this for a fact."

Thanasis was shaken from his rage when Basil grabbed him assertively by the shoulders. "What in God's name are you trying to do, Thanasis? If you don't care for yourself, at least think of your four children. What will happen to them if their father spends the rest of his life behind bars? So just stop this nonsense, and let's go and phone the doctor."

They walked silently for a while, Basil's flashlight revealing the narrow path ahead of them. Soon they were joined by Alekos Tsipras, a professor of literature and Polyxeni's cousin, who was rushing toward the Gumas house and had been coming from the opposite direction.

Thanasis said nothing and hardly noticed when Basil stopped to exchange urgent words with the professor. He continued on toward home, leaving the two men behind.

"I'm going to get the keys to the store," he muttered.

The errand took only a couple of minutes, and soon he was returning on the same path where he had left Alekos and Basil, who were in the midst of an animated conversation. Basil tried to silence Alekos as soon as they spotted him.

"What did you bring from your house, Thanasis?" Alekos asked sternly. "Show me."

Thanasis produced the keys. He was still livid, but he had left his gun at home.

By the time the three men returned to the Gumas courtyard, two young village men had left on horseback. Their first mission was to instruct Papazois to come to Panayota. Their second was to continue on to Krokylion, the bigger village, to fetch the doctor and the police.

Panayota, her eyes rolling and her face growing paler by the second, was fast losing consciousness as she lay bleeding on the ground. It was doubtful she felt the presence of George's sister beside her.

"My little bird," said her sister-in-law softly, "It won't be long now. The doctor is coming. He's going to make you better, and you'll be up again in no time. You'll see. Everything's going to be all right."

Panayota half-opened her eyes and tried to speak, but no words came forth at first. With great effort, she raised her head. Every ounce of strength she had left was spent whispering something to George's sister. She then fell back, dead before her head hit the ground.

"What did she say?" someone whispered.

"'You have devoured me,'" someone else answered.

Her remark, difficult to understand in any language other than Greek, meant two things: Panayota felt she had been killed like a gazelle being devoured by a lion, and she was attributing her violent death not to George's sister in particular but to her sister-in-law's family. In other words, she finally understood what Thanasis had been telling her all along—that George had been conspiring to murder her.

Thanasis noticed that the villagers who had gathered in the courtyard were eyeing with suspicion Vas, who had just arrived. Vas, though, seemed unaware of the attention directed his way. He was focused keenly on Panayota, helping solicitously with all that was being done for her.

Just then her mother arrived in the courtyard. "Let me get to her!" she cried. "Let me get to my child!"

Thanasis and the others parted to make way for Skevi, and she hurried to her daughter, now motionless and lying still in a pool of her own blood, her lifeless body crumpled in a heap at the foot of the stone wall.

Thanasis's sister Aggelo held Skevi as she knelt down beside her daughter, no doubt hoping to help in some way.

The old lady shook off all the helping hands and grabbed her daughter by the shoulders, pulling her up into a sitting position.

"Get up!" she shouted. "Get up, you!" She shook Panayota's body. "Breathe! Breathe! For God's sake, breathe!"

She finally loosened her grip on her daughter, and Panayota's body fell back against the ground with a sickening thud. The grief-stricken Skevi then tore at her clothes and rolled on the dirt next to her dead daughter.

As he looked away from the spectacle, Thanasis caught sight of his sister moving her hands to her ears to shut out Skevi's pitiful wail.

Nearly two agonizing hours had passed since Mother and Father had rushed outside to find out what was happening, and my brothers and I were still in bed. Finally, Aunt Aggelo arrived with her son and our cousin in tow. It was closing in on one o'clock in the morning. My brothers and I dashed to them.

"Aunt Aggelo!" I said. "Where is *Baba? Mama? Giagia?*"

"Your parents and your grandmother have gone to the Nitsoses' house," our aunt answered calmly. "Children go back to bed. You and you" she ordered pointing at her son and me "can sleep in your parents' bed. And you," she said pointing at my brothers, "can sleep in the children's bed. Now get into bed, all of you."

We did as we were told.

"Look," she said while tucking in my cousin and me, "I've got to go. All of you stay here and get some sleep. It's still early."

As soon as she left, my cousin and I disappeared under the covers, making sure to tuck them in on all sides so there were no cracks and no danger could reach us.

"Aunt Panayota is dead," he told me. "They took her dead body on a cot to the Nitsoses' house." Two years older than me, he spoke with an air of authority. "Vas killed her."

"Now they will get him," I offered.

I had heard my father speak about Vas before, but never in a flattering way. Some in our family speculated that Vas had been

91

the informer who had led the Nationalists to our relative who was killed during the civil war.

The heat from the blankets over our heads was nearly suffocating, but we didn't dare throw them off, for fear of what lay out there in the dark. If someone as beloved as Aunt Panayota could be murdered, we worried that no one was safe.

CHAPTER 15:
THE POLICE WANT YOU

I WOKE UP THE NEXT morning to find my cousin still asleep beside me in my parents' bed. But he didn't stay there for long. Aunt Aggelo entered quietly a few minutes later and carried him away without waking him. Afraid to be alone, I crept into the other bedroom where my siblings slept and squeezed myself between them.

My parents finally returned at seven o'clock, well after sunrise, but Thanasis didn't stay long. Polyxeni followed him like a shadow, watching his every move, until he finally rode off toward the direction of the family fields. Then she came back inside and met my gaze.

"Where did Baba go?" I demanded. I couldn't understand why she looked so apprehensive. He went to the fields nearly every day.

"To our fields," she answered matter-of-factly. "Now come and help me."

She was already getting breakfast ready for the children, the rest of whom were still asleep. The verger was ringing the bell again at St. George. As the last solemn echo died out, I resumed my interrogation.

"Mama, did Aunt Panayota die?"

Polyxeni hesitated. "Yes," she finally said, "she did."

"Vas has killer her, Mama," I said, assuming the voice of someone well-informed on such matters. "Now he'll see what the police will do to him."

Polyxeni frowned. "I don't want you to repeat that—ever. The police will find out what there is to find out, and they'll deal with it. All right? Now be a good boy and go to the spring and get me some water."

I grabbed a metal bucket and started up the path toward the spring, coming closer to a policeman who was guarding the murder site.

"No, no, not this way," he said, holding up both hands. "Go back," he ordered. "Back! Back!"

I reversed directions and started walking through my family's fields, but I found another policeman standing guard. After making another detour to avoid him, I managed to reach the Gumas's house, which had served as a second sanctuary of sorts for me. Whenever I was in trouble for fighting with one of my brothers or for firing my slingshot at something I wasn't supposed to shoot, I retreated there where I was always welcomed by Aliki, my maternal grandmother.

The courtyard was utterly still. Part of the wall above the sloping yard looked as if it had been scrubbed clean and stood out from the dusty remainder. Below the wall was a moist patch in the dirt, fast drying up, including a tiny red stain that someone had missed. No doubt hearing my footsteps on the path, my Uncle Gumas, the policeman, emerged from the house to greet me. He seemed to have aged overnight and moved with slow shuffling steps to a stool in the yard. I watched as his head drooped in fatigue, only to suddenly snap up as he spied something on his feet. He hurried inside and then returned a moment later with a pitcher of water, and I suddenly realized what he'd noticed.

"Lukas," he said, his words slurring with fatigue, "pour this for me, will you?"

I emptied the pitcher over his feet, my hands shaking, too afraid to ask whose dried blood I was washing away.

As Thanasis rode into his fields, he felt a sense of homecoming. He had spent his childhood there, working in the fields or shepherding the family's flock.

It felt good to be alone. Polyxeni had been hovering worriedly over him since last night. He assumed she'd spoken with Basil or Alekos, either of whom could have told her about his outburst last night. He had cooled down considerably since then and had no intention of blowing George's brains out. In fact, he'd already seen the local police chief, who had set up next door to George Nitsos's house. Thanasis had been the first to present himself in the early morning. During the meeting, which had been guarded, he had inquired about the impending arrival of the captain of the county police. He'd said little else, for he had no wish to tip his hand to the chief, a friend of George's.

Soon he arrived at the Takis's and Mary's field and, after dismounting, walked to the threshing floor of their hut, where he saw the couple sitting with their backs against a stone wall. Piles of corn kernels sat in front of them.

They looked surprised by his appearance and exchanged glances before standing up to greet him.

"*Kalimera,* Thanasis!" Takis said. "What brings you our way?"

Thanasis swallowed twice. "That bastard killed her last night," he said at last. "It's happened. You told me this would happen, and now it's happened. And I couldn't do anything to stop it!"

Takis's jaw fell open. "Linatsas," he whispered. It was a statement, not a question.

"Yes! And I'm here to ask you what you're prepared to do for Panayota," Thanasis responded. "Will you tell people what he said he would do?"

"When did this happen?" Takis asked, ignoring his question. "Where?"

"At the brook, next to the Gumas house last night as they were walking back home from the Zakkases."

"Did he do it himself, or did he find someone?" Takis asked.

"No, somebody else did it. Nobody knows who. I'm here to ask you what you will do now. Are you going to let everyone know that he tried to hire you to kill her because I'm going to give your name to the police, and they might ask you directly."

"We will," Takis answered. "Of course, we will."

Thanasis, exhausted to the bone, nodded and turned on his heels. He was back at the village by nine o'clock and Mother once again began shadowing him.

"Go and play somewhere else," she told us.

We watched as she and Thanasis spoke in whispers, eventually moving their conversation to their bedroom. When they came out a few minutes later, they both seemed changed. Mother was no longer warily following him everywhere he went, and he was suddenly more attentive to the rest of us.

I asked him if the police would arrest Vas.

"Listen," he replied, "your mother told you already that they will not arrest Vas. It is not your job to find out who killed her. It's a job for the police."

Later that morning, the captain of the county police arrived followed in the early afternoon by the major from the state police. They ordered their men to collect all shotguns in the village and then to move to the village school and conduct any interviews or interrogations there.

Thanasis was the first of the villagers to show up at the school and give a statement. After waiting at a student desk in the big hall, he was escorted into the teacher's room, which had been converted into what the villagers would soon be calling an interrogation chamber.

The local police chief introduced him to the county police captain. "Thanasis Konandreas, partner of George Nitsos," the local police chief said. "He would speak only to you."

"Well, I'm here now," the captain said, "and you may speak to me."

Thanasis didn't waste any time on pleasantries. "George Nitsos murdered Panayota," he said and proceeded to give the chief of police the names of a few villagers. "He asked all of these people to kill her, but they refused. I know Nitsos didn't fire the shots and that he himself was wounded. But I think one of these men might have done it."

He then listed a handful of potential henchmen, including Socrates, George's right-hand man.

"Interesting," said the captain. "And I take it you don't think, as many in Kupaki do, that Vas shot the Nitsoses."

"That's correct," Thanasis said. "Vas is just someone with whom Nitsos has been cultivating a feud in order to point the finger at him when the time comes. It's a clever idea of his to lead the investigation away from his own men."

I was home by mid afternoon when Polyxeni approached me.

"Lukas," she said, "will you go find out if your grandmother wants something to eat or drink?"

"Okay," I said and trotted out the door.

I didn't think much about the request until I entered the viewing room and was instantly overwhelmed by the violent stench of rotting flesh. The early afternoon heat had had a profound effect on Panayota's fast-decomposing corpse, which had been severely disfigured not only by the multiple abdominal injuries sustained in the shooting but by the autopsy that had followed.

It took me several minutes to stir up the courage to approach Grandma Mia, at the moment lost in another of her dirges. When I finally found the nerve to go through with it, I had no choice but to stand beside her and wait until she had finished another round of mourning, and as I stood there waiting in that crowded, oppressively hot room, surrounded by burning candles, I knew I would never forget the horrific stench assaulting my senses. Decades later, I would see my share of death and tragedy as an emergency room physician. But none of my future encounters would wring my insides the way that did.

To this day, I can still smell the all-permeating stench of decomposing flesh—and the various perfumes the women wore in a vain effort to smother it. I can still hear the rising and falling of grief so raw it sounded like it came from beasts, not humans. From that day on, I knew what hell sounded like—and what it smelled like.

When Thanasis asked Socrates to dig a grave for Panayota later that afternoon, several of us kids in the village followed him down the cobblestone path as he walked with a pick and shovel slung over his shoulder downhill toward the cemetery. It would be a brutal job in the afternoon heat, the kind of job only someone with great physical strength and stamina could tackle. Most of the able-bodied men in the village were too overcome with grief to oblige, but Socrates, forever cold and tough, had agreed to it. Like the rest of us, he probably had no idea that Thanasis had reported him to the police only minutes earlier as a possible suspect for Panayota's murder.

When he passed the section of trail where Panayota had been shot the night before, he didn't so much as pause. Soon we were at the cemetery, from where nearly the entire village was visible. The nearest house stood four hundred yards away. It was here that most locals were buried, typically in the same location as their ancestors. As a result, bones and skulls often came up with the earth after the digging began. A pine casket would then be lowered into the six-foot-deep grave, to be covered by a mixture of old bones and earth.

I watched with both curiosity and dread as Socrates, sweating profusely under the sun, reached a depth of roughly three feet, at which point his shovel began to fill up with old bones, as well as dirt. Availing himself of the age-old gravedigger's humor that helps a person cope with such work, he tossed a few pieces from old skeletons toward us.

We took off in headlong flight, screaming all the way, but stopped after only a few feet and returned. Sheepish, but giggling with the thrill that accompanied our fright, we bolted once more when Socrates hurled more bones our way.

As he continued to dig, Socrates began to entertain his young audience with terrifying tales of skeletons and ghosts. He told us about voices he heard in the remote hills when he was alone tending to his sheep. And we stayed on, preferring his ghoulish fantasies and the levity that unaccountably accompanied them to the real-life gloom that had overtaken our village.

At about half past five, a man shouted for Socrates from the village, his voice echoing off the surrounding hills. "Come here! The police want you!"

The voice, despite the attendant echoes, was easily understood.

"What did you say?" Socrates hollered back.

This time the voice was louder. "The police want you to come here!"

Socrates's already swarthy complexion darkened as he climbed the mountain of freshly excavated dirt next to Panayota's grave, the soft earth giving way while the old bones cracked beneath his boots. He was now towering over us children and facing the village as he cupped his ears in an effort to make out what the man was saying.

"He says the police want you!" a few of the kids dared to say.

He swallowed awkwardly and with apparent difficulty, clearly dehydrated.

"The police need you!" we screamed in unison.

Socrates cupped his mouth to relay a message to the village. "They want to talk to me?" he shouted. "What for? I'm busy here!"

"They want to talk to you!" came the reply.

Socrates was hesitating. Someone from the kids murmured, "Can he hear?"

"His ears must be blocked with the dust digging graves!" another one commended.

After a long pause, Socrates asked, "Who wants to talk to me?"

Once again, we answered as a chorus. "The police!"

Finally convinced it was time to leave, he shouldered his tools and walked back to the village, and we followed. The scene could have belonged to the New Testament, with Socrates posing as Christ, and the rest of us playing the part of his beloved children. Reality took a different route, however, when Socrates was interrogated and forced to spend the night at the school's apothiki, a temporary jail, along with two other suspects, both men Thanasis had named. Socrates's gun, we soon found out, was the only one in the village that smelled of powder, indicating that it was the only one recently fired.

CHAPTER 16:
A VILLAGE DIVIDED

Just before noon on Tuesday, less than forty-eight hours after Panayota's murder, the belfry at St. George came alive with the solemn tones of church bells. We were being summoned to Panayota's funeral procession.

As the villagers left their houses and began to gather out front of the Nitsos house, Panayota's mother continued to wail incessantly for her daughter.

An eight-year-old classmate of mine was also crying. She was George's niece, and she wept outside the school building where her father was being detained. Her cries gnawed at me.

"*Baba, Baba,*" she wept, "come home."

Her father was being detained because Thanasis had named him as a suspect. Fortunately, he and another man Thanasis had fingered for the murder would soon be released. The police were slowly narrowing their focus to two men: George Nitsos and Socrates Karaiskos. The predictable result was that our village was being divided into two camps: those that were certain George was guilty, and those who, because of blood relations or close friendship, did not want to believe it.

After the service at the village's church, the procession moved on to the cemetery looping around the policemen who were guarding the school. Through the large window of the school hall, I caught a glimpse of the interior. George, who was not given permission by the police to join the convoy, was sitting with his head on a desk slumped over like an old dog.

Following the burial, the villagers dispersed quickly, no longer willing to contend with the hot early afternoon sun. They did so in two distinct groups, each whispering amongst themselves as they walked back to the village. One group consisted largely of the families and close friends of George and Socrates. The other, bigger by far, was made up of the rest of the villagers, most of whom had already tried George and Socrates in their minds and had doled out their punishment: ostracism.

Not long after the burial, Socrates appeared outside the school with several policemen guarding him. He was asked to fire several shots into the ground with his gun. Afterward, rumors began to circulate that the police, with their special investigative tools, had been able to confirm that Socrates's shells matched the one found at the murder scene.

I had always looked up to George Nitsos. Slender, handsome, charismatic, he was the embodiment of power. Over the years, he'd worn many uniforms, whether for the civil government or the military, and he'd always worn them like a second skin, like he belonged at the top. Socrates Karaiskos, too, had long been the object of my boyhood veneration. If George was the brains between them, Socrates was the brawn. Lean but muscular, he was stronger than anyone in the village. He was the man with the gun, a reputation he had built from the days of the civil war and later as a hunter. His steely eyes and deadly aim were at once awesome and intimidating.

But the day after the funeral, as I watched three policemen remove both men from the school and start them on the trail that led out of the village, I couldn't help noticing how suddenly puny they looked.

"They are taking them to jail!" my friends said excitedly, not caring if the two prisoners heard them or not. "They are taking them to jail in Krokylion!"

Papadia, Papazois's wife, was comforting her Aunt Skevi on the front stoop when the entourage passed the Soulias house.

"You must tell them what you think of them," Papadia

urged her impatiently. "Curse them for stealing your beautiful daughter."

But Skevi, timid by nature and undoubtedly hoarse from wailing for nearly three days straight, said nothing.

The procession was nearly out of earshot when Papadia took it upon herself to give the alleged killers a rude farewell. "I curse you both!" she screamed shrilly, her voice easily loud enough to reach the surrounding hills. "I hope you rot where they're taking you. Never come back!"

George and Socrates continued on the trail toward the ragged horizon, and as they slowly made their way along the dusty path, I felt a strange mixture of happiness and disillusionment. On the one hand, I was glad to see Aunt Panayota's killers being taken away. But on the other hand, I had lost more than my aunt; I had lost a hero in George Nitsos, who had always been kind to me and appreciative of my help at the store. He encouraged me to be a doctor, promising help in the process. I wished vainly that I could somehow rewrite history so that Panayota had survived and Vas had been responsible for the shooting and dragged away.

Four days after Panayota's murder, Thanasis met with two of George's relatives, along with Papazois and another man, to prepare an inventory of the store. Now that the business partners were avowed enemies, it was only logical that their assets should be split.

At the store in the meantime, many of the usual faces were conspicuously absent. The relatives and friends of George and Socrates, most of whom lived in the upper part of the village, had begun to patronize a smaller store in the village. Kupaki would only grow more divided in the coming weeks and months.

Not long afterward, we were picking corn at out fields with Takis and Mary helping my parents trying to catch up with the harvest. I did my part by bringing fresh drinking water in a pot from the local spring. I followed the adults from terrace to terrace as they filled their aprons with ears of corn and then emptied them into burlap bags.

"Better dead than divorced, Panayota," Mary said, quoting my murdered aunt. "Better dead than divorced."

"Better dead than divorced," the others repeated.

Many women in the village had begun to remember things that Panayota had said and done, often launching into a fresh round of tears.

It was mid-September now, and the days were growing cooler. The nights, meanwhile, were longer, which only played into my fear of darkness, which seemed more acute since Panayota's murder.

Every night, as soon as darkness fell, the Nitsoses' dogs, missing their masters, would race over to the brook where their mistress had been shot and began the most pitiful howling, often not stopping until dawn. Although the Nitsoses' doors had been locked and the yard gate sealed, their dogs hadn't given up on the hope that Panayota would someday come home. With our bedrooms facing the opposite side of the brook, there was little we could do to escape the noise. The barking was worse for our neighbors who lived directly next door with their bedroom facing the brook. The dogs maintained their vigil until Panayota's memorial service, which Papazois presided over at the church forty days after the murder.

"Panayota's spirit was unhappy," the neighbors said. "That made the dogs unhappy, too."

About three weeks after the murder, the police brought George and Socrates back to our village in order to reenact the crime.

When the reenactment was over, the police asked us children to fetch them some water. I took them a pitcher, while others brought water to George and Socrates.

Moments later, George, holding a glass, approached me. "Hello, friend," he said.

I ignored his greeting.

"How are you, my friend?" he continued, undeterred by my silence. "Has school started?"

I stared silently at the man who I was certain had killed Aunt Panayota.

George Nitsos, dashing and charismatic leader of men, fumbled for something to say. Gone was the self-assurance, the charm. Never before had he looked so at a loss for words.

He glanced around uncomfortably, as if searching for an escape route. "I'll help you become a doctor when you grow up," he said softly. It was a familiar phrase, often repeated in the good old days when I had looked up to him with nothing but admiration. Now the words were spoken just above a whisper.

The idea of becoming a doctor certainly appealed to me, but I could no longer take pleasure in George's friendly banter.

I turned on my heels and walked away, George's voice growing faint behind me.

CHAPTER 17:
A PISTOL IN THE POCKET

With the arrival of October, villagers were busy completing their chores before the autumn rains began: plowing fields, collecting firewood, chestnuts and walnuts and repairing their roofs.

Polyxeni needed to do more than her share of this work and also take care of the store as her husband was away from home. Thanasis was traveling to meet with attorneys and other key people related to the investigation. Polyxeni was also concerned about family finances even though James, Panayota's brother who was now living in Australia, recently sent a check for one thousand dollars and promised to be accountable for all future expenses.

Also weighing heavily on Polyxeni's mind was a rumor in the village that "Thanasis had gone too far and had better watch out". The families and friends of George and Socrates were circulating it. "Was Thanasis safe traveling alone to other villages and towns?" Polyxeni was asking herself.

Polyxeni's anxieties for her husband's safety heightened even more after a letter came from Thanasis' oldest brother who was living in the USA and operating a bar in Saginaw Michigan.

The letter recounted an incident that happened to him a month before Panayota's murder. He'd been involved in a violent altercation in his bar which resulted in him being stabbed in the chest by a troublemaker. Subsequently, he had been arrested for shooting and killing his attacker. He was later released and cleared of all charges but the legal expenses, combined with his decision to sell his bar and move to nearby Flint in order to ensure his safety had left him just shy of destitute.

Polyxeni wasn't the only one worried about Father. Grandma Mia, too, was watching out for him—and asked me to be her eyes and ears when she couldn't be near.

"Lukas," she said one morning, "I want you to be with your father when he locks up the store at night. Can you do that for me?"

"Yes, Grandma," I answered proudly. It felt good to be recognized as being capable such a responsibility.

"And walk home with him afterward?"

I nodded in the affirmative once again.

At the store, men, most of them older, were gathering to talk and play cards. They sat on straw chairs and were slouched around round metal tables. Several community announcements hung by tacks from the smoke-jaundiced walls, which had been whitewashed years before. A wood-burning stove, in the middle of the store, provided the heat. Other than a counter and a few shelves stocked with goods, the only other items of interest were a telephone and a radio, both battery operated.

Along with selling cigarettes, groceries, and other merchandise to the customers, I brought playing cards to the men and prepared their drinks. Worry beads softly ticked against one another as cards hit the table with a competitive thump, backgammon sets clattered, and stories were told about George and Socrates in years gone by and wars in which the men had fought and travels they had made to America and other faraway lands.

As the murder investigation continued, our teacher encouraged us to concentrate on our schoolwork.

"Do not get caught up in other matters," he cautioned us one day in class. "You are here to study."

The speculation and verbal exchanges, however, continued in secret.

"They are guilty," a classmate whispered. "They will pay for it."

"You're wrong!" another shot back. "You'll pay for the injustice!"

Soon my classmates and I were solidly divided into two camps: one on George and Socrates's side, and one on Thanasis's. The division in our school was merely a reflection of the village at large. There were those who supported the accused, and those who wanted to see them put away for good—or worse. Those in between were few. Of those who pretended to be neutral, many did so only to avoid being dragged into the affair. In their minds and in conversations with those close to them, they held much stronger views.

The very geography of the village conspired to accentuate the rift. In the area in the upper part of the village, known as "Nitseika," or the Nitsos Neighborhood, lived all those who either bore the name Nitsos or were at least related to the Nitsoses in some way. Their neighbors also supported Nitsos, who was popular among them. The central and lower parts of the village, which consisted of about two-thirds of the population, supported Thanasis.

While the men from the Nitsos Neighborhood congregated in a smaller village store, those from the central and lower parts of the village frequented our store. The women from each group, meanwhile, avoided each other when they went to collect water from the springs or wells. Amongst themselves, though, they sustained a constant news network, supplying each other with the latest information on the murder investigation.

The divide even extended to *Nyhteria*, the nighttime drop-in visits so integral to Greek rural culture. Now when villagers stopped in after dinner to chat, joke, and enjoy chestnuts, feta cheese, and wine around the fire, they did so only amongst families of the same faction. It had become unthinkable to celebrate name days and other occasions with the whole village attending. Sometimes a child would sneak to the opposing side for a piece of cake, but otherwise the opposing factions kept clear of each other, even at festivities.

Papazois struggled to maintain neutrality. The cracks in the church's stone walls were finally about to be repaired, but new fissures were now appearing among the congregation. As a Greek Orthodox priest, Papazois's first inclination was to leave men's affairs to men. But he inevitably began to speak out in support of Thanasis, his brother-in-law, sparking outrage among George and Socrates's supporters.

Midway through November 1953, Polyxeni, Aunt Aggelo, and Mary were summoned to the public prosecutor's office, where they were expected to give their statements. Thanasis accompanied them to the prosecutor's office and then left to see his attorney.

As Polyxeni and the others waited in the lobby outside the interrogator's office, a middle-aged man approached Mary, and beckoned her to join him in the hallway to discuss something personal. She left the others but didn't walk far enough to keep their conversation out of earshot, for Mary was hard of hearing and forced the man to speak loudly.

Polyxeni, suspecting something was afoot, warily traded glances with Aggelo. She then cocked her head slightly toward Mary and the man talking several feet away. Although she was unable to make out everything said, it sounded like the man was trying to convince Mary to say something to the interrogator. Polyxeni glanced from the two talking furtively in the hallway to her sister-in-law, whose wide-eyed expression suggested she'd heard the same thing.

"Let's tell Thanasis," Aggelo whispered.

When Mary returned, her round face was contorted with tension, worry lines arcing across her forehead.

"I see you have secrets with male friends in the big town, Mary," Aggelo quipped. "An old sweetheart?"

Perfect! Polyxeni thought. Aggelo had managed to pry—but in a lighthearted way.

"That was a man from the village where I was born," Mary fumed. "He was trying to make a deal with me."

"What deal?" Polyxeni and Aggelo asked simultaneously.

"Nitsos must have sent him. He was offering me Nitsos's fields, the house in Kupaki for me and my family to live in for as long as we wish, and all the livestock Nitsos owns in partnership with Thanasis. I have needs, but he can keep it all. I don't want my soul to burn in hell forever."

Later that month, Thanasis was returning from his fields at dusk one day when he stopped at the village spring for a drink of water. After quenching his thirst, he leaned against a large stone and closed his eyes, the trickling water from the spring and the rustling leaves of the beech trees nearly lulling him to sleep.

A moment later, he opened his eyes to see George's older sister, standing just a few feet away.

"Hello," she said coolly.

"Hello," he replied.

Suddenly her face burned pomegranate-red, and he could tell she was gathering the courage to say something she knew he didn't want to hear.

"You know my brother is innocent, Thanasis," she said, "and if it's money you're after, just stop going after him. Just drop the case, and we won't let it go unrewarded."

Thanasis locked eyes with her. "You know your brother is guilty. I'm not selling the blood Panayota and I shared. You can keep your reward."

The woman took two steps backwards and then stopped and turned toward Thanasis. "You're not going to be able to touch George!" she screamed. "You might just share Panayota's fate!"

Thanasis opened his mouth to reply, but she scurried away before he could muster a single word.

From that day on, he began carrying a Savage .32 caliber pistol.

When Christmas finally came that winter, the village was hardly in a festive mood. After the traditional service, we gathered outside the church to exchange greetings and wish each other a merry Christmas.

Papazois, as usual, was out front shaking hands, but he, like everyone else, looked stiff and uncomfortable. He had asked me to assist him in the customary blessing of the homes in the village, and after we began our rounds in the lower part of the village, I couldn't help noticing the pensive expression on his face, which even his white flowing beard couldn't disguise.

We were halfway up the cobblestone path outside George Nitsos's house when Papazois, appearing lost in thought, jerked to a stop.

Weighed down by all my altar boy paraphernalia, I stumbled into him, unable to stop in time.

"Sorry" I said, embarrassed.

"It's all right, son," he replied absentmindedly. "My fault." He was staring at the black linen banner, fixed to the balcony railings, which read PN (the initials for Panayota Nitsos) in white letters.

Had she still been alive, Panayota would have invited us inside, offering us a warm welcome, music, and plenty of good food to taste. She would have encouraged us to rest before we continued our climb.

Papazois heaved a heavy sigh and then proceeded next door to the home of Nitsos's cousin.

She and her husband welcomed us inside, and after Papazois had performed the blessing ritual, they invited Papazois to join them for meat, feta cheese, and red wine around the fireplace.

The adults talked a while before Panayota's murder was brought up. "As our priest," the woman asked, wiping away her tears, "what are you going to do for two innocent people in jail?"

Papazois frowned sympathetically but said nothing. It was clear he had hoped to avoid the subject altogether.

But she pressed on. "This issue is dividing the village," she said, "and the priest has the moral responsibility to intervene. You need to talk to Thanasis. You must stop this avalanche, or it will lead our village to destruction."

The old priest, no doubt sensing there was no escape, finally offered a reply. "I'm the priest of everybody in Kupaki," he said, carefully weighing his words. "I try not to take sides, but I hear what even George's relatives are saying about this. They openly talk against him and call him a wife murderer."

The woman's eyes narrowed angrily.

"Of course," Papazois added, "I take nothing without a pinch of salt, but Panayota is dead. I did not hear her voice next door today. She lies in St. Anthony Cemetery. Somebody has killed her. What do you say to that?"

The mere mention of Panayota's name was enough to send a fresh round of tears streaming down the woman's cheeks. Her husband reached over to comfort her.

"I will try to keep an open mind and see what comes of all this," Papazois concluded before standing up. He motioned to me to follow and started toward the small porch.

"Have a good night and many years!" George's cousin called after us. "I'm sure our bishop also will want you to keep an open mind!"

The bishop had a fierce reputation among the priests in his jurisdiction. Was she insinuating she would complain to him? Papazois either didn't grasp the thinly veiled threat or simply didn't know how to respond to it. He led me into the cool night air without offering a reply.

Winter came and went, and by mid-May of 1954, the school grounds and adjacent churchyard were teeming with construction laborers hard at work on rebuilding the church's cracked stone walls. My classmates and I participated as did every able man and woman in the village-wide effort.

Basil, an attorney and notary public, the kind and thoughtful uncle of my brother's friend, oversaw the project and coordinated the activity.

One night Basil visited the store, and Thanasis, certain that a testimony from Basil, an educated and reputable man, would be indispensable to the prosecution, asked him to come to court as a witness.

Basil responded that he did not believe he was needed since there would be many other witnesses from the village, and it would be better for him to pretend to be neutral so the work at the church would not be affected. He wanted to keep the communication lines open with Nitsos and his family in an effort to get the funds for the repair of the church that Nitsos was holding. Basil, Thanasis realized, was trapped—and unwilling to break loose.

Thanasis knew that many in the village took his side and regularly cursed Nitsos for holding on to the church construction fund as well as for the fatigue the volunteer workers were suffering. Others mockingly stated that George would be released from jail and not only return the church's money, but also singlehandedly finish the job.

Of course, there were those, mostly relatives and friends, who kept quiet on the issue or were openly defensive. "If you think you're going to find them guilty," they would say, "you're fools."

"But they are guilty," others would respond, "are they not?"

George's defenders invariably repeated themselves: "If you think they'll be found guilty, you're fools."

Their certainty left Thanasis feeling uneasy. What did they know that he didn't? Would George find a way out of his predicament? Had he already?

Meanwhile, the latest letter from James, Panayota's brother in Australia was full of bad news: James's restaurant wasn't doing well and he would no longer be able to contribute money to the legal fund, at least not anytime soon. The letter, like the oppressive heat of May, knocked the wind out of Thanasis. His wife Polyxeni wanted to know how Thanasis was going to pay all the legal fees and save money for his children's educations.

Preparing for the worst, Thanasis traveled to Athens and asked his brothers-in-law, the Gumases, about a short-term loan so he could pay some of the legal fees, but they were unable themselves to lend him the money. Instead, they offered their house in Athens for some of the prosecution witnesses from Kupaki to stay in during the trial, which was a great help.

CHAPTER 18:
EVENTS BEFORE THE COURT

WHILE THANASIS WAS IN ATHENS, life went on back home in Kupaki, where in the middle of the wheat harvest, George Nitsos's sister had managed to get a signature on a blank sheet of paper from the son of Takis and Mary.

Thanasis did not find out about this paper, which became a letter with information damaging to him, until several months later in court.

Upon his return, he needed to focus on the worry lines on his wife's face that he'd never seen before. In typical fashion, she said nothing of her problems. If he was the loud one in their relationship, she was the proper one, the placid one. She never complained, never raised her voice to her husband. None of her family ever did, but often their silences or their soft-spoken reproaches made a man feel guiltier than if accusations had been shouted at him.

Thanasis, hoping to diffuse the tension, thought over how to approach her. She saved him the trouble the next morning as they lay awake in bed.

"Thanasis," she said softly, "do you know you go away these days, saying that you're off to the next village and will be back in the evening, and the children and I don't see you again for three or four days? Then we hear from others who saw you in other towns farther away, and they say you're so lost in thought that you don't even see them pass you.

"This village was the safest place on earth for me before all this happened. Now I live in fear daily, worrying about what is happening to you and what will become of the education of our children when all the money we have been saving is spent in court.

"Your mother is getting harder and harder to please, and I simply haven't got the time anymore. She shouts, 'Murderers!' whenever she sees any relative of Nitsos or Socrates. You know how I detest a scene. To add to all this, my older brother writes such depressing letters from Korea. In his last letter, he says, 'Don't become a widow, little sister. Before it's too late, ask your husband to stay home and end his adventures with the law.'"

Thanasis knew her brother, an Air Force officer stationed in a war zone, saw little reason to be hopeful. He was daily experiencing the horrors of the Korean War, which Greece, as a member of the United Nations, had joined.

"Polyxeni," he said tenderly, "four more months—that's all it will take for all our troubles to be over. All our lawyers assure me that it will be a straightforward win for the prosecution. Trust me."

"From your mouth to God's ear, Thanasis!" She crossed herself. "St. George, make that come true."

Thanasis, too, crossed himself, and as he did, he felt a pang of guilt. It had been far too easy to give his wife hope—the very thing he was in danger of losing.

The school year was already behind us by early July, when the vacationers began to arrive at our village. My friends and I chatted excitedly to our Athenian counterparts about the latest news from the capital. Soccer matches sprang up suddenly in open fields and courtyards all over Kupaki. Handshakes, hugs, kisses, backslapping, hearty welcomes, lingering farewells—all were the same as usual. The shadow of the murder and impending trial, however, loomed everywhere, unspoken yet ever present.

We had been transformed by Panayota's death and the subsequent divisiveness, no one more so than Skevi, her mother.

When she opened the door one day, she was shocked to see George Nitsos's two sisters standing on her front stoop.

"We won't ask you how you are," one of the women said. "We know you must be feeling what we all feel—only worse. How can anyone who knew Panayota ever forget her?"

Her sister nodded gravely.

Touched by their sincerity, Skevi broke into tears, and the two younger women began consoling her. She invited them inside; hospitality demanded it. Indeed, she couldn't have possibly turned away a friendly visitor on her doorstep, but in her grief, she let slip more than one barbed comment about her visitors' brother, instantly regretting each slip of the tongue.

To her surprise and relief, the two women didn't take offense. Instead, they deposited on her kitchen table several bags containing rice, sugar, coffee, and Turkish delights, among other items.

"*Efcharisto,*" was all she could say as she meekly accepted the gifts. "Thank you".

After the two women departed, Skevi told her neighbor and niece about the visit.

"What kind of business did Linatsas's sisters have with you?" Papadia demanded. As Thanasis's sister, it was clear she considered Skevi's acceptance of the gifts an affront to all those who had sworn to bring Nitsos to justice. And as Papazois's wife, it was obvious she felt she had the moral right to speak her mind. "They brought you presents and you accepted them?"

"I didn't want the food, Papadia," a confused Skevi replied, determined to defend herself. "But I am too old to learn how to turn people away from my door and spurn kindness with a slap in the face."

"Some people become more and more foolish the older they get!" Papadia muttered on her way out. "The Lord didn't hesitate on the high mountain to tell Satan what to do with his gifts!"

Late one afternoon, just after siesta, Thanasis visited his friend Alekos Tsipras, whose house was a short walk from the store.

Alekos, a philosophy teacher, was the one on the night of the murder who wanted to see if Thanasis had brought the store key or a gun to kill Nitsos from his house. Soon the two men were joined by some visitors from next door, and they all sat down to drink coffee. It wasn't long before they were discussing the murder and the upcoming trial. None of the men bothered to lower his voice—or curb his profanity directed at George Nitsos.

The front door of the house next door opened, and George's cousin appeared in her apron. "Says Thanasis Konandreas!" she scolded the men after marching out into her front yard to confront them. "So, what is the need for a trial in Greece, eh?"

"Why are you so het up young woman?" Thanasis retorted. "All the fair-minded people in the village have no doubt they're the murderers."

"The people of the village," Alekos said and motioned to the other men in his front yard, "all of us know it."

"All I am saying is that you should wait for the court's decision and not be prejudiced," the woman responded. "Thanasis had his trial and was found guilty, after he beat up the other village men, and we don't call him a criminal. You call us murderers before the decision."

"Even every single child knows who the murderers are," Alekos snapped. "Even those like you who pretend they don't know. Please go back inside your house. Don't let's make a scene now."

After the middle of August, there were many departures by the vacationers, who were ready to return to Athens. Their departure, however, was balanced by the arrival of several newcomers to the village. The newcomers liked to visit the brook where Panayota had been murdered, the church, the village square, the general store, and the Nitsos and Zakkas houses. They belonged to two distinct groups, and we could easily tell them apart.

Members of the first group looked sophisticated but austere. They never smiled. They wore neck ties, carried leather handbags bulging with papers, and spoke and were friendly only to a few while treating others with hostility. The village dogs ferociously attacked them from the moment they arrived and didn't let up until they had departed. They were attorneys hired by the defense or the prosecution.

Members of the other group dressed flamboyantly, carried cameras, which hung from their shoulders, and smiled, joked, and spoke with everyone. They even tried to touch and play with the friendlier village dogs after realizing the local girls were beyond their reach. They were journalists from the Athenian dailies, court reporters with a special interest in whatever bits of gossip they could extract from the locals.

PART III

CHAPTER 19:
COURT OF HONOR
AND CONSCIENSE?

ON MONDAY, OCTOBER 18, 1954, Thanasis and more than fifteen other prosecution witnesses were sitting in a chamber in the courthouse in downtown Athens, each lost in their own thoughts. Some paced nervously. Others traded small talk to quiet their nerves.

They had arrived the day before, and more than half of them stayed at the Gumases' house, some bedding down on the floor, where they would sleep for the next week or two while waiting to give their depositions in court.

Thanasis had gone to court once before and knew well what he was up against. So long as he told the truth, he told himself, he had nothing to fear. In fact, that simple fact gave him great strength. He had only to be his usual, personable self. Nothing less. Nothing more.

The trial had convened just minutes earlier. George and Socrates—had arrived with their defense team of five attorneys. The jury, ten strong, had already been seated.

"Intentional murder, illegal bearing of weapons, illegal use of weapons..." After the public prosecutor had reeled off the charges, Skevi, Panayota's mother, had appeared with two attorneys.

Socrates's handcuffs are removed as George, center, looks on.

Several minutes went by before a bailiff appeared and motioned to Thanasis to follow him back to the courtroom. It was his turn.

Thanasis stood up, straightened his gray-and-white-striped tie, which matched his solemn gray suit, and followed the man into the crowded courtroom, that was now eerily quiet. Walking in the opposite direction was Skevi, Panayota's mother—all four feet, two inches of her. It was clear she'd given the court an earful about the defendants. Her grief, still palpable, weighed heavily on everyone.

Thanasis noticed the leading defense attorney, giving him a skeptical once-over as he took his place behind the witness stand. He knew the type: cagey, tough, relentless. He was wary of the attorney, but not intimidated.

"Thanasis Konandreas," he rasped, "is it true that you once beat up a man in your village?"

Here we go, Thanasis thought. He had assumed the defense would go after his past. But he had nothing to hide. In fact, the experience had taught him much. At that trial so many years ago, his defense attorney had maintained that no one had spotted him anywhere near the other men who had been beaten. There had been no witnesses. But the court had seen through his attorney's strategy and found him guilty nonetheless. Wiser and older now, he knew truth was on his side this time.

"Yes," he answered matter-of-factly, "that's true."

"And is it true that you served time in jail?" the attorney drew out the last four words, making sure no one in the courtroom failed to grasp the importance of what he was saying.

"Yes."

The attorney puffed up with pride at the excited murmuring that followed amongst the spectators. "So let me get this clear," he said. "You assaulted an innocent man and served time for it?"

"No."

"No? You were sure that you served time for assault just a moment ago, and now you're sure you didn't?"

Thanasis knew the attorney was trying to lay a trap for him, but he also knew a way out. He turned to the Judge. "May I explain this?"

"Proceed," the judge said.

"I spent six months in jail in early 1934," Thanasis began. "My family was targeted by another family that owned property near ours because of property disputes and rumors that a Konandreas man had had a relationship with one of their girls a long time ago. The father of the girl filed several lawsuits against me, falsely accusing me of allowing my livestock to trespass into his fields. I approached him several times and told him that I respected him and his family and that I should not be personally targeted as revenge. Despite my pleas, he remained hostile.

"Then one night rustlers stole several of his animals, and he accused me of the crime and of directing rustlers to his flock. Preliminary investigations followed, and the matter would likely cost me and my family substantial aggravation and expense.

"One day at our fields, my sheep were near that man's fields, and I went to chase them away before they crossed into his property. He then started stoning me and would not heed my shouts to stop. I had to defend myself and a brawl ensued. I don't quite remember how the fight started. I lost my temper and when I calmed down, I found that, because I was younger and stronger than he was, I had badly beaten him.

"The matter went to court. Though I was cleared of the charge of rustling, I was convicted for assault. This is a matter I am not proud of, and I have always felt regretful about losing my temper, though I was badly provoked."

Thanasis took a deep breath and realized the courtroom had fallen silent once again.

"Counselor," he said, looking directly at the interrogating attorney, "I made that mistake twenty years ago, and I've paid my debt to society. And this trial is for the murderers of Panayota, not for me."

The judge then asked Thanasis, to talk about the day of the murder. "That day the Zakkases, did not invite Panayota to dinner when she visited them earlier in the evening. After leaving the Zakkases, she stopped at a neighbor's house on the way home and got some tomatoes for the dinner that she was going to cook. Later, Nitsos got his sisters to ask Panayota to join them for dinner. It's clear that Panayota had no idea this was going to happen since she had given away her flashlight to her shepherd. She was heard telling her sister-in-law that she had just come from their house and didn't understand why she should go back again."

"Nitsos arrived at the village church next to Katina's house" Thanasis added "on that day when it was still light outside. When he left, it was still not dark. He reappeared at the Zakkases' only about an hour later—well, not less than half an hour later.

During that time, Nitsos had sex with Katina in the open, next to the church."

An incredulous Judge raised his eyebrows. "If, as you say, Nitsos had prior knowledge that his wife was going to be murdered in three or four hours' time," he said, "would he have been in the mood for that?"

"Yes, Your Honor," Thanasis answered. "A selfish and shameless man — shameless to the bone like Nitsos — would be. In my rage, I would have killed him that night," Thanasis continued. "I was going to get my handgun. Basil calmed me down and stopped me."

"Instead of killing his wife, could Nitsos have divorced her?"

"No" Thanasis replied, "Panayota used to threaten Nitsos that she would kill him if he divorced her. Nitsos was afraid. He would have known that she wouldn't go that far, but he would have also known that she would make his life with anybody else miserable. Panayota was very formidable when she wanted to be. Kupaki is a very old-fashioned community and would have been on Panayota's side had Nitsos divorced her. He would have lost the status he had in the community."

"You told the court that Panayota was a formidable woman. You have told us that when she got hold of a letter Nitsos had sent his girlfriend, she went to the public square and read its contents out loud to all who cared to listen. You have also told the court that you warned her about her husband's intention to kill her. Why then did she do nothing?"

Thanasis needed only a second to mull over the question. "She didn't believe that he would go that far."

A prosecution attorney joined in to play the devil's advocate. "Nitsos wears a black tie even today, and besides his wedding band he also wears the victim's wedding band. Is this the behavior of a man who wished his wife dead?"

"It's hypocrisy," Thanasis replied. "It makes me angry."

"Suppose that Nitsos did ask Socrates to kill Panayota," the defense asked. "Why would Socrates do that?"

Thanasis answered with a question: "Who knows what Nitsos promised Socrates?"

As the cross-examination continued, the attorneys began to go after each other and soon their argument degenerated into a shouting match.

When order was restored the defense asked Thanasis if he was an active member of a left-leaning organization and a vocal supporter of Communist ideology during the '40s. The defense protested, saying the question was irrelevant, but the judge ruled that Thanasis should answer.

"It's true that I joined the leftist organization you are referring to," Thanasis answered. "But so, did Nitsos, and so did almost all the men in Kupaki at the time. We wanted to fight the Germans and the Italians, not to bring Communism into our village. I was never a Communist."

"You were a business partner of Nitsos, were you not? And is it not true that the livestock and the store you jointly own are worth a fortune?", the defense asked.

Thanasis laughed. "The store and the livestock are worth very little, and that's nowhere near a fortune."

After the court was adjourned later that afternoon the strapping lead attorney for the prosecution approached. The attorney, who stood a good head taller, wrapped Thanasis in a bear hug—an unprofessional but much-appreciated gesture.

"What am I to say but 'Bravo, Thanasis'? I was sitting there feeling like I was being slowly roasted over a coal fire. I could have kicked myself for not preparing you better for this sort of thing. But you're a natural. You began turning the whole show around right from the time you came clean about your criminal record. If a jury loves anything more than an honest witness with no criminal record, it's an honest witness with a criminal record who appears reformed and repentant. It gives a sense of purpose to the whole business of passing judgment."

The policeman Gumas, the next witness said, that he was the

first to arrive at the scene of the shooting, and he had found George Nitsos lifting his wife's dress to examine her injuries. He told the court how he had carried the injured woman to his yard and how, during that time, George had offered no help.

Soon after Gumas was back in his seat, Thanasis turned to his attorneys. "Look at the jurors," he whispered in an urgent tone. "Look at them huddled in those three groups. There are seven over there to the left who seem to be the defense's people. There are two with their heads together to the right who don't seem to care at all. And what about the one on the front lower right, who completely avoids the others? And look at that lot in the front row. If they are law school students as they say, I am Alexander the Great. They act like public relations workers for the defense. I don't like this one bit. Do you think we'll get a fair hearing?"

Thanasis was already convinced that some newspapers, particularly the *Acropolis* and the *National Herald*, were mouthpieces for the defense. A cousin of George Nitsos was the editor of one of the Athenian dailies; it was likely his opinion was influencing other journalists.

"Let's wait and see," the attorneys replied calmly.

Takis, the next witness said his family worked for George Nitsos, and gave a detailed account of the various proposals Nitsos made to him and his wife through the years, all associated with rewards, to murder Panayota, and how he was able to avoid it. He spoke to Thanasis Konandreas, he added, because he was close to Panayota and close to Nitsos as his partner and able to keep an eye on him. Nitsos also sent him messages from the jail and offered him money if he didn't testify today.

The defense attempted to portray Takis as a Communist, something that infuriated the prosecution attorneys. They told the judge that the defense, was using untrue accusations about the alleged political affiliation of the prosecution witnesses Konandreas and Takis. They asked the court to either prohibit such tactics or give them the right to submit evidence that Nitsos had leftist sympathies.

"The prosecution's statement has been noted," the judge said.

Before Takis was done, the defense presented a letter allegedly written and signed by Takis's son. The letter said Takis had been persuaded by Konandreas to give false testimony incriminating Nitsos. In return, the two would share the livestock that was now jointly owned by Nitsos and Konandreas. Takis expressed utter surprise that his son could have written such letter. His wife Mary, who came to the witness stand later, told the court that her son had only signed a blank sheet of paper months before and flatly denied that he has written such letter.

The judge turned to the jury. "This court is unable to judge this case without an examination in court of additional witnesses. The conflict we just heard about over the letter allegedly written by the son of the last two witnesses illustrates that need. In addition to their son, I have a list of seven more potential key witnesses. The bench is asking the jury to postpone this case for those witnesses to be summoned."

The prosecution supported the proposal. The defense opposed it.

After a brief deliberation, the jury foreman announced, "With honor and conscience, we say there is no need to postpone this case."

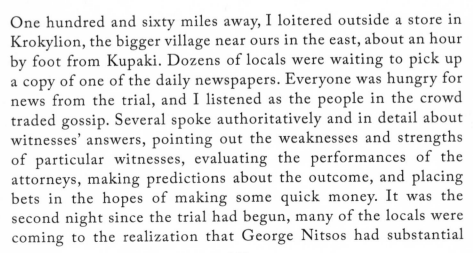

One hundred and sixty miles away, I loitered outside a store in Krokylion, the bigger village near ours in the east, about an hour by foot from Kupaki. Dozens of locals were waiting to pick up a copy of one of the daily newspapers. Everyone was hungry for news from the trial, and I listened as the people in the crowd traded gossip. Several spoke authoritatively and in detail about witnesses' answers, pointing out the weaknesses and strengths of particular witnesses, evaluating the performances of the attorneys, making predictions about the outcome, and placing bets in the hopes of making some quick money. It was the second night since the trial had begun, many of the locals were coming to the realization that George Nitsos had substantial legal support and might just escape conviction. Many who had pegged him guilty before the trial were suddenly adopting a neutral stance, or even coming out in support of him.

After working my way to the front of the line, I bought a newspaper and then started for home. I wasn't the only one. A throng of locals were returning to Kupaki and other nearby villages, newspapers fanned out in their hands. The ones I recognized from Kupaki, who belonged to the defendants' faction, were carrying the *Acropolis* and the *National Herald* while I and the others didn't have a particular preference, carrying whatever newspaper was available at the store.

Once back at the village square in Kupaki, I watched as the locals crowded around my new teacher, to hear him read aloud the latest news. A few minutes later, the discussion moved from the village square to our home, where Mitros, Thanasis's uncle, squared off against Grandma Mia. The two had never gotten along, at least not while I'd known them. For some reason, Grandma took it as a personal slight that Mitros and his wife had never had any children. Likewise, she disapproved of his gambling habit. He was a great card player — but never knew when to call it quits.

Though illiterate, Mitros possessed a great deal of judicial wisdom. Known in the village as the "illiterate attorney," he was always right in predicting the outcomes of cases involving land or water rights disputes, or issues over village animals' damage to crops. Now, he was predicting that the trial would end without resolution.

"*Periplanumeni,*" he said. "The trial will end in *periplanumeni.*"

He repeated the catchword relentlessly until finally Grandma Mia had endured all she could take.

"Can't you just tell us in plain Greek what that means?" she snapped.

"Well," Mitros said, clearing his throat, "it's not easy to explain it accurately to someone with no legal knowledge, but the closest meaning of *periplanumeni* in simple words is 'a case that is not won, but not lost, either.'"

"Bah!" Grandma snorted. "What on God's earth does it mean? In jail or free?"

The onus to explain fell upon my older brother. Wanting no part of the argument, he wisely passed the burden to me. "You explain it," he said casually.

I thought a moment. "I've only heard that word in connection with the Gypsies and the Jews, Grandma," I said. "It's like saying, 'lost, moving, chased around without purpose...' You know—like being without a country or a home."

Grandma Mia groaned. "Can nobody speak plain Greek anymore? Gypsies and Jews indeed! What have they got to do with that kiaratades who killed my poor Panayota? Nobody tells me if he'll be in jail or not."

My reputation as a good student was saved a day or two later when the school teacher confessed to Mia that he himself had never heard the word used in relation to a court verdict.

"Mitros!" she grumbled. "He must be going soft in the head and who will look after him in his old age now?"

Mitros, when he heard about her comments, was equally dismissive. "Empty-headed old bat! And her grandson and his teacher! Empty heads, the whole lot of them!"

The next witness, Father Papazois, walked confidently to the stand as if he were there to address a congregation. The stunning contrast between his white beard and the neck-to-toe black vestment and his black stove pipe hat made an immediate impression on the crowd. He smiled benevolently at the judge, the jury, the attorneys, and the crowd that stared at him.

Papazois told the court that, with the exception of close friends and relatives, everybody in the village thought the accused were guilty.

The defense accused the priest, who was a relative of Konandreas, of testifying so that Konandreas would gain financially if his business partner Nitsos was out of the picture. The priest denied such favoritism and then told the defense that their claim that Thanasis was a communist was baseless because he himself came to Athens when these allegation about Thanasis were made and met with authorities who were responsible for such decisions and asked for the basis of such action.

"There was nothing incriminating Thanasis, and the decision by the local Kupaki Nationalists force was overruled." Papazois concluded.

One juror asked, "Upon your priesthood, Father, do you take upon yourself that with all you know, the accused are guilty and have committed the crime?" "Yes, I do," Papazois replied.

Before Papazois left the stand, the prosecution read a letter sent to George Nitsos by his father who was living in America. In this letter, George's father, responding to news about his son's marital problems, advised him to get a divorce.

The defense responded by reading a letter sent from Nitsos and Panayota to Nitsos's father, where they stated that there was nothing wrong with their marriage and that anything he may have heard to the contrary was "mere gossip by envious people."

Ntinos, another prosecution witness, known in the village for his sense of humor, told the court that on St. George's Day, shortly before the murder, he visited George's home with a few friends to wish him many happy returns of the day, and they all saw him swear at Panayota and hit her—right there in front of everybody. "I left the house without eating any of the cake because of that." He shook his head ruefully. "And the cake did look very good."

He added that he was never aware of any beatings by the police at the school in the village where the accused were kept after the murder and finished by saying that Nitsos's double play with both Nationalists and Communists during the civil war resulted in one year of exile for him by the Nationalists who ultimately prevailed.

Vas, the next witness, said that the night of the murder he was home sleeping, and he woke up because of the noise outside.

When a neighbor told him that Panayota had been shot, he knew that Nitsos was behind it. When he arrived at the Gumas house, Panayota was dying, and he heard nothing from her.

"Why did Panayota accuse you of shooting her before she died?"

"Nitsos must have told her that in her vulnerable state, and she must have believed it. Nitsos needed an enemy to blame, and I fit the bill perfectly. I was an outsider with no support in Kupaki."

"What about your relations with Konandreas?" the attorney asked.

"They're not good," Vas answered, "because he thinks that I led the detachment during the civil war that killed his relative."

Polyxeni Konandreas, the next witness—a pretty woman of medium height and solid build without seeming to be obese—carried herself with poise, coming off as taller than she really was. Laconic, private, naturally persuasive, uninterested in gossip, she made her listeners feel that here was a woman who could never lie.

When she told the court that she was asleep at the balcony of her house when the gun shots were heard, a juror, asked: "What kind of work did you need to do in the middle of the night that took you to the balcony of your house at the time of the murder?"

It was the same juror that had asked many questions to Polyxeni's mother Aliki, who became confused with delicate time matters during her deposition earlier and forced the public prosecutor to intervene. The prosecution had already marked this particular juror as very partial for the defense and branded him as the defense's "6th attorney".

"It was summertime then," Polyxeni said simply, "and we do sleep on our balconies during summer in our village."

Following that Polyxeni said that she and Panayota were good friends "I knew Nitsos was treating Panayota terribly, ridiculing her in public for the littlest thing. He was always creating episodes to belittle her. I have heard him call her

132

'whore' and other things that I am too ashamed to repeat in court. I told him if he were my husband we wouldn't have lived an hour together."

The next prosecution witness, who was Mary's brother said, that in 1946 his sister visited him and told him that Nitsos had sent her to ask if he was willing to kill Panayota for forty gold sovereigns. He cursed her and sent her away. He then told Thanasis, who he knew was close to Panayota, and he would have reported the matter to the local police, but the police had been disbanded because of the civil war.

Back home in Kupaki, I continued to read the newspaper to Grandma Mia and Uncle Mitros. As I read beneath a kerosene lamp, every word was commented upon or contested. When I quoted testimony from the prosecution witnesses, my two elders cursed the defense attorneys for their statements. When I mentioned people from the village who supported the defense, their names were met with an uproar, with my brothers and I unleashing sarcasm and Uncle Mitros swearing aloud.

Grandma Mia, meanwhile, would react the same unforgettable way each time. First, she would ask me to reread the passage referring to the defense witness's name and views to make sure she'd heard everything correctly. But she would never wait for me to finish. She would wave at me to stop, then she would stand look in the direction she thought the home of the person in question, and unload.

"Na, na, na, na... you..." From there, her vocabulary shrank until only epithets, physical handicaps, intellectual deformities, and cruel gossip were hurled at the defense supporter and every member of his or her family.

Once finished with her tirade, Grandma Mia would turn around, sit down, and ask calmly, "And then what does it say?"

CHAPTER 20:
THE MISTRESS AND THE DEFENSE

KATINA, GEORGE'S MISTRESS, APPEARED YOUNG and vulnerable on the witness stand at first, but soon she was answering questions with a mixture of naiveté and a shrewd artfulness beyond her years.

In high school she needed a guardian, and she sought and received the supervision of George Nitsos, whom her father thought of as a reputable person.

She wanted to get her high school diploma first and then immigrate to Canada, but she had been afraid she would never graduate, because George Nitsos was on good terms with her teachers, and he would have kept her where she was. Nitsos was telling her that it was better to become a teacher in Greece than a cleaning woman in America. He took her immigration papers from the postman and did not give them to her.

She did not let George have sex with her at first, but later she did because she wanted his protection. Nitsos wasn't the first man she had sex with, but another man two years before. Since Nitsos was not going to leave his wife for her, she didn't feel she was causing problems in his marriage. Nitsos used to tell her that Panayota was smart and a good housewife, and she would never accept any unkind things that people told her about him. Nitsos bought her small presents like a watch or left her some money when he was visiting her in school.

She was not afraid of pregnancy because he told her he was careful. While going with Nitsos, she did not have sex with other men. He never asked her to marry him, and she never asked him to marry her. In fact, Nitsos told her that he would help her find a good husband.

She met Nitsos outside the church in the morning the day of the murder and again that evening, during which time Nitsos wanted it all done in a hurry.

"What did he want done in a hurry?" she was asked.

"I can't say that here in front of all these people. He... you know..." Katina's voice dropped to a nearly inaudible level. "He wanted... satisfaction."

"Do you mean sexual gratification?"

"Yes," she stuttered.

"Did he threaten you with dire consequences if you let the secret out?"

"He didn't threaten me. He only said that I shouldn't talk about this." Katina appeared to suppress an involuntary shudder. "Even if someone asked me with a knife to my throat or removed all the teeth in my mouth."

"Are you sure he was not referring to the murder of Panayota that he was planning?"

"No, he never planned with me to murder his wife. He was talking about situations like my father finding out after Effie saw us kissing and Marula told his wife."

She was home, Katina continued, when the murder took place, and the next morning Konandreas told her that they had arrested Nitsos as a suspect and that the rumor in the village was that Nitsos had said many things to the police about her and that she should plan what to say. He suggested that she accuse Nitsos in revenge for all that he had done to her.

At noon that day, Katina continued, the captain took her deposition, and she kept her word to Nitsos not to tell him about her relationship, but when she found that he had already spoken about it, she had no choice.

"The captain threatened me," Katina continued, "so I said some of the things out of fear. Later he also told me that nothing would happen to me if I said whatever I wanted to, so I said some things because I felt revengeful toward Nitsos for saying all those things about me".

After Katina was done, her cousin told the court that he spoke to her after the murder and she told him that she was going to retract a prior statement she had made against Nitsos because she was in love with him, and he had promised in a letter sent from jail to marry her when he got out of jail in three years. When he asked her if she was going to marry a murderer she replied that Nitsos didn't pull the trigger himself.

Polyxeni returned to the village after about two weeks in Athens, and my siblings and I were surprised with several school supplies, including a handful of ballpoint pens with the letters BIC engraved on them, which we'd never seen before. We were so excited to experiment with our new pens that we hardly noticed Uncle Mitros and Grandma Mia behaving amicably as Mother gave them first-hand news of the trial.

"Thanasis and his attorneys don't think that Nitsos and Socrates will be out free," she said, "but they think the court may find the case *peplanimeni.*"

At the sound of the word, Mitros and Mia exchanged glances.

"What did I say!" Mitros cried, nearly jumping for joy. "What did I say! And all these empty heads here thought I was mad."

Grandma Mia could only snort in derision.

"That's exactly what I've been telling them all along, Polyxeni dear," Mitros continued. "And they all drove me crazy, including that moron of a teacher."

"Papu," I said, joining the conversation, "you were saying *periplanumeni*, not *peplanimeni.*"

"Ha!" an overjoyed Mia shot back. "This is what comes of bandying about big words without even learning to read and write."

"What difference does it make if they both mean the same thing?" Mitros said defensively.

Mother tactfully changed the topic and went on describing how the defense had prevented any additional witnesses from appearing for the prosecution.

"The jury agreed with them," she said. "One of the jurors came forward and announced, 'With honor and conscience, we have decided that there's no need to postpone the case by bringing in additional witnesses,' and the prosecution attorneys began to—"

"Honor and conscience, eh, Polyxeni?" Mitros said, interrupting. "What a joke!"

Nitsos's shepherd, testifying for the defense said, that he was in his hut located about one-and-a-half hours by foot from the village. Socrates, who was at a nearby hill with his lambs, called out to him about midnight or a little after and asked him to come and keep him company. Socrates couldn't have gone to the village to kill Panayota and be back by then. He then said that Socrates's gun was old and useless, but when challenged, he couldn't explain why with the same gun, Socrates was able to kill a partridge the same day the murder took place.

Nitsos treated Panayota with respect, he continued, and gave her more freedom than other men in the village did with their wives, for example, letting her play cards with him at the store.

When the prosecution read this witness' initial deposition, which was very different from what he was saying now, he replied that the police did not read back to him what he had said and that they could have changed it.

The next defense witness, said that he was asked by the police captain to compare the shell found at the crime scene with one Socrates was asked to fire as a test the day after the murder, and the two did not match.

When asked why the police captain, who was on good terms with Nitsos, would incriminate him and why the captain, who had several policemen with him, asked his help when he wasn't even known to the captain, he replied that he did not know.

Another defense witness accused Vas of bad conduct during the civil war and during his tenure as a field warden. That conduct, he felt, made Nitsos go after him constantly, increasing the animosity between them. Vas, he said, could have hired someone to try and kill Nitsos.

Zakkas, George's brother-in-law, the next defense witness, said that the dinner in his house on the night of the murder was not a last-minute decision, and the women in his house had planned this much earlier. It was Panayota who decided, he continued, the time they left.

At the Gumases' yard, he added, George helped dress Panayota's wounds before he fainted from grief. He was never told by either George or Panayota that they had marital problems.

"Panayota had eight cousins?" the defense asked, "Do you know if any of them except Thanasis Konandreas has sought to take Nitsos to court?"

"No. And that proves that Konandreas is motivated by selfish interests, and not by love for a cousin, which the other seven cousins surely also feel. Konandreas may have been secretly jealous of Nitsos because he was always second, as was the case with the church council," Zakkas concluded.

Nitsos's sister took the stand next and said, that George had nothing to do with making the plans for dinner at the Zakkases. She said that she was with Panayota the whole time after she was carried to the Gumases' yard, and she never said, "Now that you have devoured me."

Nitsos's first cousin who lived next door to the Nitsoses, said that she had never heard George and Panayota arguing or become aware that Panayota was not sleeping at home.

Before calling the accused on the witness stand the judge asked the jury once again to postpone the case in order to summon new witnesses, but the jury again denied his request.

Due to holidays occurring in the next few days, the judge adjourned court for several days. When the court reconvened,

Demosthenes Dapontes, the lone juror Thanasis had pegged as impartial, asked to be excused due to illness. With no alternate juror to take his place, the court had no choice but to accept his request and prolong the recess. Though this delay did not allow the court to summon the seven witnesses they wanted, it did allow them to summon the state police major and forensic specialists.

The state Police Major said that by examining the guns owned by the people in Kupaki, he found out that only Socrates's gun smelled of powder indicating that it was recently fired.

Also, the shell from the crime scene matched the shell from the test firing done with Socrates's gun. The major dismissed the possibility of someone placing a shell at the crime scene to incriminate Socrates because the crime scene had been guarded. In addition, he said, someone would have needed a shell from Socrates's gun which was unlikely.

The major admitted that not checking the shell found after the murder for fingerprints was a serious omission.

He added that it would have been easy for Socrates to clean the powder from his gun after he killed the partridge, but perhaps he didn't expect his gun to be examined closely, or he wasn't thinking straight. As to why Nitsos and Socrates did not remove the shell after the shots were fired, he said that in the darkness perhaps they couldn't find it or they didn't have enough presence of mind at that moment to even look for it. Three forensic experts for the prosecution and one hired by the defense took the stand next.

The experts argued a lot, but by the end of the day, they agreed on two things: the shell had come from Socrates's gun, and it would have been impossible for the killer to miss George and hit Panayota if the intended target had indeed been George.

Thanasis, meanwhile, met one night with his attorneys to discuss his biggest fear: a rigged jury.

"They have twice," he began, "refused the judge's request to postpone the case. What does that mean to you? And they act and ask questions like defense attorneys. Do you need more?"

"We must be patient," one of the attorneys counseled, "and focus on the positive."

"What about the juror who claimed illness?" Thanasis countered. "By doing so, he gave the court the time to seek more witnesses. What does he know? What does the court know?"

The two attorneys traded wary glances. Thanasis's concerns were impossible to ignore. So, too, was the political climate around them. In post-war Greece, you could never be sure of a fair deal—unless you knew the right people.

The three men began preparing a list with the names of all the jurors. Then they began to study several variables for each juror: the village or town he hailed from, his family and clan loyalties, his workplace, his current neighborhood, and his political affiliation. Could they encourage any of them to reconsider their verdict? If all else failed, Thanasis and his attorneys agreed, there was always plain old money, whose color often changed the tint of people's perceptions.

The attorneys highlighted the names of two jurors on the list. Of everyone on the jury, the two men seemed to be keeping their distance from the majority.

"You've got to pull any strings you can to make sure these two jurors' minds aren't swayed by the defense," one of the attorneys said.

Thanasis frowned. "I don't have any connections in the big city except with a few *galatades* who moved here ages ago," Thanasis said, referring to the old milkmen who had decades earlier relocated from the country to Athens. "Those strings are too long to even try pulling."

"You never know," the attorney replied.

That night Thanasis sat down with his brothers-in-law to cull through their memories. Soon they were bringing up names they'd long forgotten and analyzing each man's political power, social standing in the community, and willingness to take the risk that went along with attempting to influence the decision of a court of law.

Gradually they came up with a list of four people that might be able to help them. There was Thanasis's cousin who was an attorney. Another attorney who came from Kupaki as well and was a politician and ex-parliamentarian. A medical doctor, wealthy and prominent socialite – whose house Panayota worked at in Kupaki when she met George. And a parliamentarian who was the National Undersecretary of Economy.

The challenge before Thanasis now was to persuade the men on that list to wield their influence in the service of a just cause.

The first man on Thanasis's list was his cousin who was at first hesitant to believe that the jury could be so corrupt. After Thanasis's presentation, however, he studied the list of jurors' names with concern.

"I'm afraid I don't know any of these men," he said. "Who else are you going to see?" Thanasis told him.

"The Undersecretary is a good one," his cousin said, still studying the list. "It appears these jurors are all bank employees, and their bank belongs administratively to his ministry of national economy. His father was a director of the Bank of Greece."

A few minutes later, Thanasis was approaching the ministry of finance. As he neared the building, he couldn't help wryly noting that, with the municipal elections for the new mayor of Athens in the offing, this was just the right moment to approach politicians for favors.

After looking him up and down, the man at the front desk quickly dashed Thanasis's hopes of a meeting. "The Undersecretary is mourning his mother, who has just passed away," the man said. "Besides, the minister will be busy with several important appointments in Greece and abroad as soon as he's able to return to work."

In other words, Thanasis thought, *Don't bother coming back.*

Thanasis continued on toward the city center, to the office of the attorney-Politician Ex Parliamentarian.

"Thanasis," the attorney-politician asked, "how come you're here instead of at the court?"

"May I have a word with you in private?" Thanasis asked.

"What's there to talk about, Konandreas?" he asked, suddenly switching to Thanasis's surname. "You've made an embarrassment of the village, and your trial has resulted in smearing the reputation of unmarried Kupaki girls."

"The girls you're talking about have built their own reputations," Thanasis continued, his anger building. "I have no responsibility for their fate."

Several other attorneys who knew Thanasis drew closer.

"I'm staying out of this business," the attorney-Politician declared with a wave of the hand. "I'm not talking to you. I'm not talking to the other side. If you've decided to take each other's eyes out, do so by all means, but leave me out of it."

"If that's the way you feel, then so be it," Thanasis shot back, "but do you remember how many times you've said right here in your office that they're the murderers?"

The great attorney, politician, and ex-parliamentarian, visibly reddened. "If this is all you want to talk about, we're finished! No more discussion! Not one word!"

"Right!" Thanasis snapped. "Let them out, then, free to have fun as usual, and come and see and enjoy them with pride, dancing at the village square—the ones you once called murderers!"

"Out!" the attorney Politician said "Out!"

Thanasis, one step ahead of him, was already bounding down the marble steps to the sidewalk. For once the noisy hawking of street peddlers selling pretzels, pistachio nuts, and lottery tickets sounded soothing to his ears.

Disregarding Thanasis's advice, Papazois, who was also in Athens, decided to try his own luck at speaking with the attorney Politician, but before Papazois could even make his case, he was cut off.

"I know why you're here," he told Papazois.

"Listen," Papazois said calmly, "you know Nitsos did it. You have told me so right here in your office."

"To give one's opinion is one thing, to actively take sides is another."

"I know. I know your cousin is married to Nitsos's brother, and a relationship like that is not to be trifled with, but for the soul of Panayota, I implore you to help."

The attorney fell silent. Was he reconsidering his position?

Papazois decided to press on. "As a priest, I know about forgiveness. Forgiveness is the balm for the soul that repents, not the right of every sinner. Tell me, is there anything anybody can ever do to make Nitsos repent? Don't you see what he's doing in court, accusing everybody from our village of things they've never even dreamt of doing?"

"I'm totally disgusted by the shame the trial has brought Kupaki," the attorney – Politician said, "and I want to stay out of this fight."

"Listen, Nitsos will return to the village more arrogant than ever before because he's now a celebrity—and a free one at that. And that will drive Thanasis to the edge. There's no saying how much worse that could make things for our village. Just think: punishment for Nitsos would not only be just; but it would protect our community."

The priest felt his voice falter as he spoke. It was clear he was fighting a losing battle. He continued on in the hopes of winning the man over, but eventually he found himself trudging out in defeat, his humble exit not unlike Thanasis's before him. Later that evening, Thanasis and Papazois made their way in the cool November air toward the doctors' residence. The doctor was not a politician; he was a humanist who deeply felt Panayota's loss.

"Is there anything we can do?" he asked.

Thanasis shared in detail his experience with the other three.

"Do you believe that all ten jurors have already made up their minds?" the doctor asked.

"Some of the jurors don't appear influenced yet," Thanasis replied, "which is why we're trying so hard to find someone who might be able to prevent the defense from influencing them."

"Do you know their names, their jobs, their places of birth, and so on?" the doctor's wife, asked.

"Yes", Thanasis answered. He removed the list he was working on from his pocket and handed it to the couple.

The couple studied it carefully, pausing to whisper to each other on occasion as if in church. As they traded whispers, their faces grew more optimistic. Soon the suspense was more than Thanasis could take.

"We couldn't help noticing that one of the men works at the Farmers Bank of Greece," the doctor finally said. "Her brother" he continued pointing at his wife, "is the bank director. He might be able to help with this particular juror."

CHAPTER 21:
SOCRATES' VENDETTA AND GEORGE'S ACT

SOCRATES WALKED TO THE WITNESS stand and said that on Sunday morning, the day of the murder, he was hunting, and he killed a partridge. He spent the rest of the day at his fields taking care of his lambs, and that night between eleven p.m. and midnight, he was on top of a hill, near the hut of Nitsos's shepherd. He made a fire there and went to sleep. His wife came early Monday morning and told him about the Nitsoses. At that news, he said, he left for Kupaki at once.

"But not before hiding your gun. Why did you do that?"

"When I reached the outskirts of the village, I met Takis's son. He told me that there were policemen in the village, and they were examining people's guns. I was worried that I might get into trouble for not having a proper permit. The young man advised me to hide my gun somewhere before entering the village. So, I buried it under a cedar."

He went and offered his condolences to Nitsos, and then the police chief ordered his men to collect all the guns in the village, including his.

When he told the captain that he had killed a partridge, he was told not to pluck its feathers.

In the afternoon, Konandreas asked him to dig a grave for Panayota. Then he was asked by the police to go to school, where he was arrested. The police whipped him and asked him to give

145

a false confession saying that he was the one who committed the murder.

"If the police beat you to make you sign a false confession, why did none of the villagers hear anything from the school?"

"I'm not the kind of person to scream and weep," Socrates answered. "That doesn't mean that it didn't hurt."

"Why didn't you mention this mistreatment during your initial testimony?"

"I didn't have the experience to know that I could complain."

Socrates then said that he had no reason to kill Panayota. He was an orphan and struggled to support his sisters and has always valued a family and a home. Why would he want to destroy someone else's home and family? He had never been found guilty of any crime in all his life. He had never bothered anybody. When he was made the village warden, he never used his authority to harm anyone. Only once he had a run-in with somebody, and that was with Konandreas, and that man hated him. He arrested Konandreas's son when he broke into the store and stole items. Konandreas threatened him then and said, "You'll pay for this." Sure enough, he was making him pay now.

Socrates then said that he did not believe Nitsos did it, and as to who had done it, he replied that Konandreas knew. It could have been himself or Vas or Takis or one of the other Communists. They were probably trying to kill Nitsos and killed Panayota by mistake.

When Socrates was asked to explain the fact that the shell found at the crime scene came from his gun, he said that the shell found at the crime scene was old and reloaded, and the one the captain sent to the interrogator was not. The captain must have made a mistake and mixed the shells up.

"Why didn't you make a formal complaint that the shell was not from your gun? A year has passed since you were first arrested."

"My attorneys told me that my innocence would be clear when the forensic results came out."

"You say that Konandreas has a vendetta against you," the

prosecutor began again. "But Konandreas did not even mention you as a suspect during his initial statement. And he asked you to dig the victim's grave. I cannot imagine he would be so sadistic."

"He hadn't yet made arrangements about who the witnesses would be, and that's why he didn't mention my name earlier. Now he's found people to lie for him against me. He's that kind of a man. He badly beat up a man some years back. He and I have had bad blood—everyone in Kupaki knows that."

"Listen, Socrates," the prosecutor said, "I'm obliged to point out some huge gaps in your statement, especially the fact that you haven't accounted for the time between nine-thirty p.m. and one a.m. on the night of the murder."

"Two hours are not enough to get to Kupaki and return to my hut," Socrates insisted. "And my gun that you keep talking about—it shoots wide of the mark four out of five times. Why would I depend on that gun to shoot and kill someone in the middle of the night? A moving target in the darkness, and a gun like that! If this wasn't a court, I'd think this was a bad joke."

Dressed in a light gray suit and black tie, his well-groomed hair combed back, George Nitsos took the witness stand looking as debonair as ever. Thanasis had seen his act before and was not in the least impressed by the man's outsized personality. Everyone else in the courtroom, even the prosecution attorneys, appeared seduced by the man's charm.

George gazed out at the faces staring back at him and, ignoring the prosecution's opening question, launched into a monologue. "I'm saddened," he said in a somber tone. "I'm saddened because I'm here, ladies and gentlemen, bearing the heavy accusation of being a wife-killer. This is why I ask you to listen carefully to my story—the story of an innocent man who for fourteen months has been dragging the cross of false accusation from detention house to detention house, from prison to prison.

"I come from a good family. My dream was to become a good

family man. I married my wife in 1940 because I had been in love with her since 1936. Our wedding party lasted eight days. I lived with my wife in harmony"

Then Nitsos started talking in length about his military service against the Italians and Germans during the war, despite repeated admonitions by the judge to talk about the murder on September 6, 1953. He continued elaborating about his military feats and sacrifices during the civil war, which resulted in making many Communists his enemies.

After the judge again ordered him to talk about the day of the murder, Nitsos said, "On Sunday, September 6, 1953, I went to church, and before the service was over, I stepped outside for a smoke. There Katina came to talk to me. After lunch and a nap that day and around four thirty p.m., I went to my store, and my wife followed me later. She came to tell me that they had made arrangements for dinner that night with the Zakkases. She told me not to be late. I was a little late, arriving around eight-thirty p.m., and my wife had been there and had gone home. Before she left them, she had asked the Zakkases to call her when I got there so she could return. Indeed, my sister called her, and she came back.

"We ate, played cards—we actually played *Koumkan*—and at about ten-forty-five p.m., my wife told me that she was tired and wanted to leave. I asked her to stay a little longer so that I could finish the game. After the game, I got up to leave, and the Zakkases gave us a flashlight.

"On the path on the way home, I held her beside me with my left arm, and I was shining the flashlight with my right hand.

"We walked about one hundred and sixty yards, and when we reached a curve in the path where the ravine is, we were shot at from the front. We moved backward a couple of steps, and we were shot at again. We fell down and started screaming. We were in great pain, and we were screaming, 'They're killing us!'

"They took us to the Gumases' front yard and called for a doctor. Panayota was saying, 'Vas has killed us.' I tried to help

BETTER DEAD THAN DIVORCED

her, but then I felt sick and faint, so I moved farther away, and then... she..."

What an act, Thanasis thought. The bastard was the only one from the entire village who did not cry when Panayota breathed her last outside the Gumases' house, and he was trying to do it here!

George took a moment to regain his composure in the packed courtroom, which had fallen silent in the wake of his teary performance.

"Before noon the next day, I went with the police and a doctor of forensics, who came from a nearby village to help, to the crime scene, where the county police captain found an empty shotgun shell that had been fired.

"He began examining it. The doctor told him to be careful with the handling of the shell because the murderer could be traced from the fingerprints on that shell.

"That afternoon, the county police captain called me and asked me to help find the killer. I told him that I wouldn't rest until I found the murderer. I told the police about my suspicions for Vas, and especially Poly's father."

"On Tuesday morning, while the church bells were ringing for my Panayota's funeral, the captain of the county police ordered me to go to the school. I got there as fast as I could, running part of the way. I asked the county police captain what he wanted and pleaded with him to let me attend the funeral, but to my surprise, he said that he was arresting me on suspicion of the murder of my wife.

"I said, 'Me?' And he said, 'Sit down, keep quiet, and don't even think about giving me any of your famous lip, because by the time I finish with you, you'll be as still and silent as that two-thousand-pound chest over there.'

"I was dumbstruck. Surely anybody can see that I haven't got up from a bed in a mental hospital and walked here to give evidence. I'm of sound mind. Why would someone like that kill his wife of fourteen years? If I needed to get rid of her, couldn't I just go to America where I have relatives?"

149

"Isn't it true that you prevented Katina from going to America? Does that seem like the action of a man who didn't have any deep feelings for the woman with whom he was cheating on his wife?" the prosecution asked.

"If I wanted to marry Katina, I could have done that so easily in America. And I never told Katina not to go to America. All I said was, 'Why do you want to go to America? To clean dishes?' And that has been made into a big thing here.

"When I was commander of the band in my village, I could have killed my wife a hundred times without any fear of repercussions. Why then I did not just ask Socrates then, to kill my wife if I wanted to do that?"

Following that, Nitsos attacked Konandreas, saying he got on the side of the police and he has used every underhanded trick in the book that even hardened criminals would balk at.

"It's Konandreas who is the murderer, not me," George continued. "It was he who planned to kill me. Only he ended up killing my wife.

"I want to remind you that at eleven p.m. that night Konandreas passed by the crime scene. His wife was on the balcony of their house at the same time. Why was she there? And his mother-in-law was staying up and looking out through her window. It's obvious that all these people knew something was about to happen.

"There's no doubt that Konandreas is trying to incriminate me, but I'm not sure who else is with him on this. It could be his shepherd or Vas."

"Are you not aware, Nitsos," the prosecution attorney asked, "that Vas and Konandreas are not on good terms?"

"That's true, but they're both scoundrels, and when scoundrels see an opportunity, they bury the hatchet and become partners in crime."

"Do you deny asking Takis and Mary to help you murder Panayota?"

"Ask Takis and Mary, indeed! They are such chatterboxes — worse than the radio. As the court has heard, Konandreas and

Takis are trying to take the livestock that the three of us have jointly owned."

George eyed the jury confidently before addressing the whole court.

"I challenge all those who accuse me, to find a single reason to kill my wife. They say I'm a womanizer. I'm not denying that — nobody's a saint. I certainly am not, but I'm not proud of my relationships with other women. I'm not the only adulterer in Greece. Many men cheat on their wives, but none of them leaves his wife for an easy woman. None of them would murder his wife in order to have these relationships. Punish me for adultery, not for a murder I had no hand in.

"Your Honor, respected members of the jury," George concluded, "I'm alien to these false accusations leveled against me. You see before you a totally innocent, misunderstood man who has lost the wife he loved and now pleads for his own life and freedom that his enemies have taken away from him. I request that you let me have them back. I'm innocent, and I hope you will return a verdict of not guilty."

CHAPTER 22:
THE 9:1 VERDICT

ON NOVEMBER 12, 1954, ON a cool, misty evening, Thanasis took his seat beside the prosecution and waited. The clock read a quarter past eight when the judge entered from his chambers. The courtroom, filled beyond capacity, buzzed with anticipation. Tonight, the jury would decide on a verdict. Tonight, George and Socrates would be sentenced or go free. The two men, until now the embodiment of bravado, sunk into their seats. Their anxiety was palpable.

"Let me remind each member of the jury of the solemn oath that you've taken," the judge began.

As soon as the judge was through addressing them, the jury disappeared behind closed doors to deliberate. Thanasis watched as audience members spun around in their chairs to discuss the case with others nearby. Seconds ticked by slowly, agonizingly.

Thanasis looked at Skevi, Panayota's mother, who remained in her seat. Silent, immobile—she sat perfectly still, save for her gnarled old hands, which were hard at work on a black handkerchief, now twisted in knots. Every few minutes, she paused in her work as her eyes darted furtively toward the door behind which the jury continued to deliberate.

Finally, at three a.m., after nearly seven hours of debate, the jury returned.

The jury foreman stepped forward.

Silence fell over the courtroom.

"With honor and conscience," he announced, "I declare the

verdict of the lawful majority of the jury." He paused to clear his throat.

Thanasis felt his heart race. For several days now, he had feared the jury was corrupt, but maybe he was wrong. Maybe the men had deliberated this long because someone among them had argued the facts. Maybe the truth had won.

"We find the defendants," the foreman said, "not guilty."

The people were instantly on their feet, their collective roar nearly swallowing the foreman's pronouncement. Some shouted in joy. Others gesticulated wildly from anger. A month's worth of testimony had been whittled down to seven hours of deliberation, which in turn had been squeezed into one grave pronouncement. George Nitsos and Socrates would go free.

Thanasis searched the courtroom until his gaze fell on Skevi, Panayota's mother. She was staring back at him, her eyes lost in confusion. It wasn't until she saw the look on his face—he could only imagine how disappointed he looked—that she appeared to understand what had happened. And as her countenance fell, he saw the same misery in her eyes, the same utter devastation, that he had seen back in Kupaki, in the Gumases' courtyard, on the night of the murder, when she had collapsed and tore at her clothes. She clamped her jaw shut, drawing her lips into a thin line, but was unable to stop the forlorn wail that rose from deep within her battered heart.

The moment the furor abated in the courtroom, the public prosecutor, asked the judge's permission to speak.

"Your Honor," he began, "the jury's decision doesn't agree with the evidence that came to light from detailed deliberations. I request that the court find this decision peplanimeni, so that the case can be decided by another trial at a later date, which will be determined by the attorney general."

A defense attorney shot to his feet. "We request the court reject the public prosecutor's appeal," he said. "Accepting it would be tantamount to disgracing the rule of law and the institution of jurors."

The judge deliberated for fifteen minutes, and at half-past

three in the morning, he announced the court's acceptance of the prosecutor's appeal.

A few hours later, after a fitful bit of rest, a tired and battered Thanasis dragged himself out of bed and went to meet with the prosecution team. What he and his attorneys learned after reading accounts from two different dailies only confirmed his suspicions that the jury had been corrupt.

The behind-the-scenes reporting of the court reporter for the newspaper *Vradini* showed how the jury had come to vote nine-to-one in favor of the defense—and how the defense had been privy to that information before the verdict had been issued:

The leading defense attorney carelessly revealed a secret that he wasn't supposed to know. While congratulating the jurors for their verdict, he expressed his disappointment that one juror had voted against the majority and had therefore given the right to the public prosecutor to ask the court for a hung jury. Following that, during the judge's deliberations of the public prosecutor's proposal, I was assured that the jurors made it known in the corridors of the courthouse that indeed there had been one vote for the minority and that the vote in question had been produced by the juror who was not approaching the others...

The lone juror who was not approaching the others was Demosthenes Dapontes.

"The defense attorney wasn't supposed to know that, was he?" Thanasis asked his attorneys. "Am I not correct in thinking that only the judge and the public prosecutor were allowed to know the balance of votes at this point in the trial? So who leaked the information to the defense? They must all be in cahoots with each other—the defense team and the jury. What a farce!"

"What's done is done," one of his attorneys said. "Let's concentrate on building a solid case for next time."

Thanasis sat back in his chair and let go an exhausted sigh. He couldn't imagine enduring a second trial. He was painfully aware of the pressure he would face from family and friends to drop the whole thing. Stymied by his own sense of duty, Thanasis stood up.

"Where are you going?" one of his attorneys asked. "We still have much to discuss."

"I need to telegram my wife before she hears the news from some village gossip."

At the village, while George's and Socrates's supporters celebrated the news proclaiming the two men innocent, those of us who had supported the prosecution weren't quite sure how to respond. *Peplanimeni* didn't roll off the tongue nearly as easily as guilty. Would there be another trial? Would George and Socrates ever be punished? Far from providing any sense of resolution, the month-long trial in Athens had merely given us more of what we had already endured: more questions, more indecision, and more waiting.

CHAPTER 23:
FAMILY PRESSURES

"How could those jurors overlook all that evidence and rule 'not guilty'?" Mitros kept asking.

"I wish I knew," Thanasis answered with a sigh.

"What did those wretches say?" asked Mitros, who wasn't ready to give up.

"The jurors? Well, their foreman said that 'with honor and conscience' they could say that Nitsos and Karaiskos weren't guilty."

"Honor and conscience, indeed!" Mitros spat.

Thanasis could do nothing to appease the old man. It had been the same with everyone since his return to the village a few days earlier. Family members, friends, and fellow villagers had suffocated him with their questions. All anyone wanted to know about was how the jury could have possibly come to its decision.

Gradually they had given up, but Mitros, ever dogged, had continued with his badgering. The disbelief in his tone told Thanasis that his uncle had no intention of letting go anytime soon.

On the day of Apokreon, the beginning of Advent, which followed soon, my mouth watered as my parents made preparations for a holiday feast of roast lamb with potatoes and cheese pie, all of which would be roasted over the embers of a wood fire. Also on the menu were the usual suspects: feta cheese, olives, and red wine.

Papazois and Papadia arrived with their two daughters just

before meal time, followed shortly by Aunt Aggelo and her two children. We crowded around the table, and soon we were pleasantly stuffed.

After dinner, Thanasis fed a cheerful fire another huge log. While my brothers and I played nearby, the adults talked about the good old times, before the murder. It seemed that even now, in the warmth of our home, surrounded by beloved family, none of us could escape the courtroom back in Athens. The verdict was like an uninvited guest who insisted on making his presence felt.

"Hoy, hoy," Grandma Mia said with a heavy sigh. "What are we going to do now?"

She looked at Thanasis the way Polyxeni often looked at me when she disapproved of something I'd done. "I want you to stop, to give up the trial and stay with your family. Let those bastards go to hell or wherever the devil takes them."

Her daughters Papadia and Aggelo gave encouraging nods.

"Is this what you think I should do?" Thanasis asked, clearly taken aback.

"Yes!" the women answered without hesitation.

Papazois, who had been silent so far, spoke up. "Listen, Thanasis," he said gently. "You have done more than your share. You can't leave everything else and spend the rest of your life and money in the courts."

"It's not as though you haven't done enough for your cousin," Polyxeni said, having waited patiently for her turn to speak. "But how much more can anyone expect from you?"

Father listened silently as he moved one of the logs in the fireplace with a poker.

Finally, Grandma Mia had had enough. "What are you doing?" she demanded. "Playing with the fire? Stop that right now. Say something!"

"What do you want me to say?" he asked with a shrug. "Do you want to let the bastards who killed your niece walk free? Do you want to live the rest of your life with the knowledge that you walked away from a chance to seek justice for Panayota?"

"Panayota has many other cousins," Papadia, responded. "They are men, too, and none of them has taken this to such extremes."

"We all understand your problem, Thanasis," Aunt Aggelo said. "Nobody wants to let the murderers go free, but we need to go on with our lives."

"Let's suppose I give up," Thanasis said. "Do you think that I or any of you will have peace and quiet if Linatsas comes back to Kupaki? Have you forgotten about him?"

No one uttered a reply.

"Even inside the court," Thanasis said, pressing the issue, "he was behaving in his usual devil-may-care way. Do you think a man like that will change? He will go around challenging us and mocking us, until we take the law into our own hands."

Mother's face darkened. "Look," she said, pointing at my siblings and me. "Look at these children when you feel all that pride and bravado and vengefulness. Don't you realize they'll become orphans and you'll be in jail? Go! Go after those killers if you have to—and be a killer yourself!"

"Do you really think I enjoy this?" Father asked meekly.

"Well, if you don't," Papadia said, "why don't you just stay home?"

Thanasis dropped the poker with a clang and sank into his chair. "If this is what you all want," he said in a defeated voice, "what else can I do? I'll simply have to give up."

Everyone seemed to be relieved to hear this, even the children, who had long ago stopped playing to listen to the conversation, but I wasn't. I wanted Thanasis to continue on in his quest for justice.

Later that night, long after the last of our guests had gone home, Grandma Mia cursed and ranted in her sleep. Like the rest of us, she was still devastated by the verdict. As someone who had once been a staunch supporter of Thanasis's efforts, she seemed to have given up on justice for Panayota—and wanted Thanasis to do the same.

Would he? Would Grandma and Mother and everyone else succeed in tying his hands? As I drifted off to sleep, I hoped somehow Thanasis would find the courage and strength to continue the fight.

Thanasis was already awake the next morning when Polyxeni began stirring.

"What we said last night can't be done," he said as soon as she was fully awake. "I have to finish what I started."

She propped herself up on one elbow and stared back at him with a faint smile that hinted at pride, tenderness and a tint of regret. "You're going to continue, right?" she said softly.

"I knew it. I know you."

CHAPTER 24:
THE ATTORNEY GENERAL

"Do you have an appointment?" an official at the attorney general's office asked. "Is the attorney general expecting you?"

Thanasis, dressed in a clean suit and standing erect in the reception office, looked directly into the man's eyes, determined to portray dignity as well as doggedness. "No," he said. "But I have traveled all the way from my village to see him."

In fact, Thanasis had been quite busy of late. While others in the village had drifted lazily toward the inevitable winter hibernation, spending the shrinking daylight hours indoors curled up beside the fireplace, Thanasis had been busily laying the groundwork for a second trial.

Although he had kindly refused an offer from Uncle Mitros to write him into his will—a generous but ultimately futile offer, considering he needed money now, not in ten or twenty years—he had written his brother in America and had received the promise of one thousand American dollars, along with a letter of encouragement containing an emboldening rallying cry: *Go after the bastards.*

He had then traveled to the courthouse in the city of Patras, where George had spent time in his youth. There he had learned that, despite the turmoil of the civil war, records still existed of George's arrest there so long ago. Next, he had met with his local attorney, and asked about George's record as well as funding for witnesses. Wasn't it possible, he had asked, to get the Department of Justice to cover his witnesses' expenses if the judiciary summoned said witnesses? His attorney, clearly impressed that Thanasis had done his homework, had nevertheless warned him that he would need authorization from the attorney general—no easy thing to secure.

Now, with Christmas just around the corner, Thanasis was standing in the attorney general's outer office and politely demanding a meeting with him.

"What's your name?" another official asked. By now, Thanasis had drawn a small crowd of curious officials.

"Thanasis Konandreas."

"Which village did you say you're from?"

"I'm from Kupaki."

"This man Konandreas came from Kupaki and thinks he can see the attorney general," a guard standing nearby said in mocking tones to his fellow sentry.

"Did you say Konandreas from Kupaki?" a man asked as he entered the building.

The guards parted to make room for the man, a middle-aged gentleman dressed in a well-tailored suit.

"Yes," Thanasis answered.

"Are you not from the big trial with Nitsos and Karaiskos?"

"Yes."

"He wants to see the attorney general," one of the guards said, "but we're trying to explain to him that that's impossible."

"Stay here, Mr. Konandreas," the official said and disappeared inside the office.

He was back within minutes. "The attorney General will see you now," he announced.

Inside the stately office, The Attorney General came out from behind his desk to welcome Thanasis with an extended hand. "A pleasure, Mr. Konandreas, a pleasure!" he said enthusiastically. "I wish Greece had more Greeks like you!"

Thanasis, surprised by the warm reception, managed to mutter his thanks and sink into the plush chair that the attorney general offered him.

"What can I do for you?"

"I'm a cousin of Panayota Nitsos, who was—"

"I know the whole case, Mr. Konandreas. Why else do you think I said I wished we had more Greeks like you? Now tell me what I can do for you."

"The prosecution needs several witnesses for the second trial," Thanasis said, still shocked that he had received such an unexpected welcome from the attorney general. "I was wondering if they could be summoned by the judiciary. You see, I have spent the best part of my meager savings on fighting this case, and now—"

"Let me have the names," The Attorney General said, interrupting him once again. "I'll summon them, and I'll ask the ministry for a special daily rate, by which the prosecution witnesses can be reimbursed for their expenses."

"Thank you."

"Is there anything else?"

"Well, there is one more thing," Thanasis answered cautiously. "I need to locate some old court records, which I believe show that about twenty years ago, when George Nitsos was living in the big city of Patras, he was taken to court for theft—and was found guilty."

The General immediately summoned his clerks. "I want all the information we have on George Nitsos of Kupaki."

While his subordinates were searching the archives, the Attorney General told Thanasis that his department had been working hard to ensure that the events of the first trial would not repeat themselves.

"We have decided to have the second trial in Halkida, where criminal justice has traditionally been strong. We have never had any problems with people playing the system there. The jury there will be beyond reproach. I don't want the trial to be in a city where the proximity to Kupaki could mean unwelcome political influence."

"I have no experience with such things, sir," Thanasis said modestly. "If this is what you think is best, I will go with it."

"Good man. I will appoint the most upright judges for the

trial and ensure that the jury will be chosen from the most educated people of Halkida, who are also economically and politically independent and therefore unapproachable by any outside influences."

While Thanasis was savoring the unexpected stroke of good fortune, the attorney general's subordinates returned to say that no records on Nitsos existed and, though they could be in Patras, where the offense had taken place, they had most likely been destroyed due to their age.

"I have been to Patras looking for that record," Thanasis responded quickly, before the attorney general could reply, "and I was told that the records from that time in 1934 exist."

"If such a record exists," the General said, "I promise you that my department will make it available at the trial in Halkida."

Thanasis thanked the attorney general and stood up to leave.

"Mr. Konandreas." the General's voice stopped him at the door. "The law will take its course, and the attorney general must remain impartial while it does, but I wish you all success. If there is anything I can do, do not hesitate to get in touch."

"Thank you, sir," Thanasis said appreciatively. "I hope your wish comes true."

PART IV

CHAPTER 25:
TO HALKIDA FOR JUSTICE?

ABOUT A WEEK BEFORE CHRISTMAS 1954, news arrived that the trial would take place in Halkida, the capital of the island of Evia.

When Thanasis contacted his two attorneys, they advised him to hire another attorney, someone from Halkida who was familiar with the court, its judges, its attorneys, and its ways.

Though Thanasis received a check for a thousand dollars from his brother in America, along with wishes for much success, he was wondering how he was going to pay a third attorney and the expenses for all the prosecution witnesses in a city which he knew nobody from the village had ever visited.

As the swallows began to fly over Kupaki signaling the coming of spring, thirty men and women left the village to appear in court. There were no additional defense witnesses, but the prosecution had five new ones. March 10, 1955, marked the first day of the new trial in Halkida, a city of 25,000 renowned for its seaside beauty.

The great Greek philosopher Aristotle had spent a substantial part of his life in Halkida, his mother's hometown, as had numerous physicists intent on solving the unique tidal phenomenon of its waters. Affectionately known as "the bride of the Evoikos Gulf," Halkida spanned the mainland as well as Evia Island and was connected by a series of bridges.

Thanasis and the other witnesses arrived early on March 10th at the courthouse, an early 20th-century neoclassical building. Ionian columns decorated the entrance, where a marble statue of Andreas Syngros, the man whose philanthropy had funded the building's construction, stood. Evergreens dotted the courtyard, as did benches, already occupied by the visitors.

As soon as the door was opened, the group moved inside, and Thanasis, one of the first to enter, spotted an enormous crucifix hanging above the farthest wall and just over the judge's bench.

The Judge called the court to order and along with the public prosecutor proceeded to select the jurors.

Ten jurors and two alternates were picked, and their ranks included four attorneys, a professional with a legal background, three industrialists, a schoolteacher, a retired police officer, a pharmacist, and a merchant. The defense team, meanwhile, was headed up by two local attorneys.

Thanasis, the first witness, strode to the front of the court in a dark jacket, white shirt, and black tie. (Photo of Thanasis at the witness stand on this day at the right side of the book cover). After repeating much of his testimony from the previous trial, he told the court that George had once sent Panayota to a nearby town and had planned to kill her en route with the help of a right-wing extremist group.

"Linatsas also tried to talk a dentist into killing Panayota by mixing poison with the dental anesthetic shot," he said. "The dentist refused and informed Nick, a dance instructor."

"Why didn't you propose this Nick as a witness?" the public prosecutor, asked.

"I couldn't get him to be a witness since he's related to Linatsas."

A defense attorney took up the cross-examination next. "I put it to you, Thanasis Konandreas, that young people have relationships that don't necessarily end in marriage. Can you explain why you felt duty bound, as you claim, to ensure that

George Nitsos married your cousin Panayota just because he had slept with her?"

"That was not the issue. Nitsos promised Panayota to marry her. She slept with him because of this promise. This was a question of a broken promise. That is why I pressured Nitsos to marry Panayota."

"I further ask you," the attorney continued "that divorced women no longer feel alienated as they used to do, even in more traditional areas of Greece like your village. Therefore, the claim that Panayota would be humiliated if Nitsos divorced her is patently a non-issue that has been made into an issue by the prosecution."

"Counsel," Thanasis said, "let's not forget that we're both from neighboring villages. I'm from Kupaki, and you're from the village across the river from mine, and you have close ties with Kupaki. If one of your city-bred colleagues had put that argument to me, I would have at least thought that they believe in that nonsense. You should know better. Tell me: how many divorced women do you know in our area who live a normal life in their communities without any alienation and humiliation? We both know the families in the area. Whisper to me if you feel uncomfortable naming names in public."

The attorney retreated, visibly deflated.

"The witness is smart," the judge muttered just loud enough to be heard.

"That he is," agreed another attorney on the defense team. "Had he not been, he would be where the accused are sitting now."

That night at their hotel, Thanasis coached Skevi, Panayota's mother, who was slated to take the witness stand the next day.

"I know you can't help feeling a little intimidated at the sight of all the slick attorneys and the judge and the packed courtroom," he said gently, "but you need to let them see how much loss you feel. You're much more than just a village woman.

Show them the strength inside you. You're a mother who lost her daughter. Let those people see how that loss makes you feel. Show that in your words. Show that in your actions."

Thanasis saw the fruits of his coaching the next morning in court, when Skevi launched into a litany of curses against George and Socrates the moment she was called to the witness stand. Several minutes were needed for the judge to calm her down, but eventually he was able to steer her toward a calmer discussion.

"Nitsos mistreated my daughter," she said, "not because she didn't give him children, but because of all the other women he was carrying on with. I saw my daughter tormented and bitter, but she kept everything inside and never complained.

"She wanted to spare me, and I burned inside because I knew what it was costing her to do that. Once in my presence, that man threw her plates and glasses onto the floor and shouted, 'If your mother weren't here, I would have beaten you black and blue!'"

Without pausing for a breath, Skevi pointed a finger at Nitsos and once again raised her voice. "You devil of... you sent her where I will never see her again! At times my daughter had to sleep outside her own house. You even brought one of your whores to that house. That was why lightning hit your house and you fell and broke your leg." Skevi turned to the judge. "And my daughter lived through all this. Kupaki is so small that everyone would get to know if she left her husband. It would have been a big humiliation to be the only woman in the village to be estranged from her husband."

George stood. "May I ask the witness a question, Your Honor?"

"Sit down, Nitsos," the judge snapped, "before you make a big blunder."

"I insist, Your Honor."

The judge, hoping to make Nitsos change his mind, hesitated while looking at him. "Are you sure?" he finally asked.

"I am, Your Honor."

"Very well, then."

"In 1944," Nitsos began, "did I not send your daughter to Athens to get treatment for her stomach troubles? Do you remember how long that was for? Would I have done that if all the lies you say about me were true?"

"You're going to ask me questions now?" Skevi shot back. "You sent her there to get rid of her, you bastard, so that you could have fun with your whores."

The judge shook his head at George. "I did tell you that you were going to make a blunder, did I not?"

In the village after the afternoon session had begun at school, I approached my new teacher with an unusual request. "My grandmother wants me to go and get a newspaper from Krokylion," I said.

No doubt eager to know the news from the trial in Halkida, the teacher didn't hesitate to grant me his permission.

I hurried home, dropped off my school bag and, after receiving two drachmas from my grandmother, raced down the steps into the yard.

"Hey, you!"

I skidded to a halt and turned to see Mitros, my great-uncle.

"If you're going for a newspaper," he said, handing me a few coins, "get me one, too."

"Grandma Mia gave me the money, Papu," I replied impatiently. I was eager to get to Krokylion before the papers sold out.

"I want my own paper," he harrumphed.

"But, Papu, you can't read. What are you going to do with it?"

"Well, that grandmother of yours can't read, either," he said grumpily.

Realizing it was foolish to argue any further, I quietly pocketed the two drachmas and took off for Krokylion.

In Krokylion, amidst the buzzing crowd at the shop, I

managed to buy copies of the newspapers *Kathimerini* and the *Ethnos*. I was back home before sunset.

Soon my brothers and I were huddled around the fireplace with our grandmother.

Mitros arrived just as we were ready to read the papers. "Where is my newspaper?" he demanded.

"Here it is, Papu," I said and handed him a paper. "But who will read it for you?"

Mitros, who hadn't been to the house since his last argument with Mia, fell silent.

Grandma, in a surprise move, stood up, grabbed a stool, and carried it to the other side of the fireplace. "Sit there," she said dryly.

Mitros hesitated. I could tell by his furrowed brow that he wasn't sure he could trust this olive branch from Grandma Mia, but he eventually accepted the offer and took a seat beside us boys. This, I knew from past experience, was the beginning of an unofficial truce between the two warring elders, and it would likely last just until the next difference of opinion between them sparked another quarrel.

We recognized the judge in a photo that accompanied one of the articles. He and the public prosecutor had been in Kupaki only a few days earlier to inspect the crime scene.

As I skimmed a section in the *Kathimerini,* skipping most of the names of the jurors and whatnot, I came to a passage about Thanasis and the answers he was giving to the judge's questions.

Mitros, though, wanted to know more about the jury. "Read that bit about the jurors to me again," he said. "Does it list their names and occupations?"

Mia, of course, wanted only to hear about what her son had said in Halkida. "No," she said. "Keep reading about Thanasis."

For a moment, I feared the two would come to blows, but just as quickly as their tempers flared, Mitros lowered his voice.

"Thanasis said they promised in Athens they will have good jurors this time. I just need to find out what sort of jury they've got there," he said in a reasonable tone.

"Fine," Mia shot back. "Go ahead, then."

"D. Tsokos, industrialist," I said, reading the first name.

"Good!" Mitros shouted his approval.

"N. Vamvakulas, merchant," I continued.

"Keep going," the old man answered.

"P. Kulopoulos, attorney."

"Yes!" he shouted.

"K. Karros, retired military officer," I read.

"Yeeeeeees!" he responded uncorking the word in one long howl. He was on his feet now, his eyes twinkling brightly. With each new name read, his triumphant shouts grew louder.

By the time I had finished reading the twelfth name, Mitros was hollering like a teenager whose favorite soccer team had just scored the winning goal at the World Cup.

"Atta boy!" he shouted. "Now we have them! Nothing can save them!"

Mia, too, was overjoyed by the news, and the two rivals began discussing the jurors and rejoicing in the hope that the jury would hear the case fairly this time, unaffected by the influence of money or politics.

"How many times have you been a juror in court?" Mia asked Mitros. "Did you talk to those judges when they came here?"

Soon our teacher arrived.

"What do you think the outcome of this new trial will be?" the teacher asked Mitros.

"I predict that we'll win," my great-uncle replied confidently. "I haven't the slightest doubt about it. What about you?"

"You could be right," the teacher replied in a cautious voice. "Anyway, I'm going to wait before I say anything."

CHAPTER 26:
"STRAIGHT IN THE VILLAGE, CROOKED IN COURT"

As the prosecution witnesses were becoming more familiar with the waterfront in Halkida, there were many occasions they met defense witnesses walking in the opposite direction along the promenade. Back in Kupaki, the opposing sides took any opportunity to have it out with their rivals, but here, in this seaside town, the witnesses appeared weighed down by the burden of representation. They were staying in nearby hotels and not only did they have to testify to the truth on the witness stand, but they were responsible for representing their village. Everything they did in the big city would reflect back on Kupaki. So, whenever the groups met they studiously avoided confrontation, limiting their interaction to harmless statements about the weather, the conveniences in their hotels which stood just two hundred yards apart from one another, and the sights of the city.

Thanasis knew the people in the city were very sympathetic to his cause. Many were stopping and encouraging him outside the court and in the streets. What was confusing him was a sad melody some young people were singing by the courthouse, which was sympathetic to the plight of the defendants:

> *Come, Mother, to see this son of yours*
> *Come, cry with him and feel his sorrows*

Within these prison walls I languish
Imprisoned by injustice and anguish

"I'm going to take this matter to my local attorney," he said. "He needs to find out who these people going around singing this stupid song are. The prosecution ought to be able to do something about this!"

Little did he know that fifty years later, on a hot August evening in Halkida's St. Nicholas Square, when I was visiting to research this book, I would encounter the very same song, this time sung for me by an old man who was a regular at the court back then.

During Takis's testimony that followed, the defense asked the judge to delay the proceedings, so they could have time to summon a villager, who had written a letter contradicting Takis.

The prosecution objected, and that infuriated the leading defense attorney. "You're denying us the opportunity to find the killer," he said. "Konandreas has committed the crime, and we're not allowed to prove it!"

"If the defense attorney knows more than the evidence has shown so far," the public prosecutor replied, "he should appear as a witness. It would be my privilege to question him then. Otherwise, he should stop scattering baseless accusations about."

The same attorney called Thanasis the murderer of Panayota again soon there after during Mary's testimony. Thanasis complained, and the public prosecutor gave Thanasis the opportunity to sue him in this present court, which Thanasis did. The attorney then accused the public prosecutor of bias. Heated exchanges between the two men followed, nearly leading to a fistfight.

A shepherd who worked for Thanasis then gave his testimony and said that the summer before the murder, he went to see George to pay him back some money he owed him. During the meeting, George offered to pay money to the shepherd instead.

"He said, 'I will give you one hundred sovereigns if you kill a person I have in my house,' and I answered, 'George, I don't do these kinds of things.' When he realized I was not the man for such a job, he replied, 'It was a joke.' A couple of months later I told Konandreas about it."

When another villager, told the court later that he had also been solicited by George to murder Panayota and spoke to Konandreas about it, the defense wanted to know, "Why did everybody go to Konandreas and not to the police when they knew Nitsos was planning the murder? And why did Konandreas himself not go to the police?"

The judge called upon Thanasis to answer.

"As I have said many times before," Thanasis said, "I didn't go to the police because I didn't believe that Nitsos was really going to kill his wife, but it was also because of Panayota. She did not want me go to the police either."

Thanasis Konandreas, left, argues with George Nitsos in court, March 16, 1955. A prosecution witness on the witness stand stares straight ahead.

"Was Panayota herself willing to help you and act against her husband?" the public prosecutor asked.

"She always wanted to work things out amicably," Thanasis explained. "She loved Nitsos, and she didn't even want to hear about divorce. She was also a bit conceited on some matters involving her relationship with her husband. To illustrate this point, I want to tell you about the time I wrote to her brother and sister in New Zealand about their problems. After that, Panayota wrote back to them saying that the things written to them were all lies. She loved that man."

"But do you see what happened in the end?" a juror asked.

"I do. Several people from the village told me to forcefully mediate a divorce. But I didn't want to be known as a man who broke up families in Kupaki."

A defense attorney joined in. "If you had told Nitsos to get a divorce, would that have been for the better or for the worse?"

"I had no way of knowing it at the time, but it would definitely have been for the better," Thanasis answered. "I would probably have argued with Nitsos and split the business I had with him, but we could probably have avoided the terrible thing that happened later."

"Were you not afraid that Panayota would tell Nitsos that you had told her that he was planning to kill her?" a juror, asked.

"No. Their relationship was like the one between cats and dogs."

Polyxeni Konandreas, spoke about the terrible way George had treated Panayota, and soon George accused Polyxeni of lying and stated that Polyxeni was working like a slave at her house while he was treating Panayota as a queen.

"If I work like a slave, I do it for my own family," Polyxeni retorted, "but you exiled your 'queen' as you are now calling her, to a place from which she will never come back!"

After Polyxeni, Vas repeated his testimony from the Athens trial.

When asked by the judge what the public opinion was at the village, he gave a simple answer.

"Judge," he said, "a case straight in the village, crooked in court."

His words were immortalized in the newspapers the next day.

Well before the end of the second trial, Thanasis was overwhelmed with financial troubles. The money from his brother from America was eaten up, and he was forced to dip into his savings since free board and lodging, as was the case at the Gumases in Athens, wasn't an option in Halkida.

He knew he wouldn't be able to pay his witnesses' expenses much longer, especially with substantial hotel bills and attorney's fees still due. He asked the witnesses to pay their own way for now, and he would reimburse them later. They all agreed.

There were moments of levity, such as when the prosecution witness Ntinos, the self-appointed village jester, staged a mock court among the prosecution witnesses while they waited in their chamber for their turn to be called to testify. Playing the judge, Ntinos appointed several of his fellow villagers as members of the court. He delighted his audience mostly with the expedience with he moved the procedure, unlike the real court that had cooped up his fellow villagers for days, confined for hours at a stretch.

Amidst all this, Thanasis had yet to find out about George Nitsos's prior conviction in his youth. Thanasis's attorneys had informed him that the court records had been found and were now in Athens, but had they been sent yet? Even with the attorney general on his side, Thanasis knew delays could occur.

When Katina's turn came to walk to the witness stand, there were people stuffed into the courtroom and the hallways, and they filled the grounds outside, where they overflowed down the steps onto the street.

There were whispers. "So this is the famous Katina?"..."Is this the woman the terrible murder took place for?"

The newspaper photographers' flashbulbs went off with high speed in high anticipation, but the court, hoping to make the young woman more comfortable, ordered the courtroom cleared. The newspaper *Acropolis* called her "the enigmatic young lover of Nitsos" the next day and pointed out that throughout her testimony, she was "shaking with sobs." Her last tryst with George was called an "orgy" at the altar of the village's church.

CHAPTER 27:
"JUST ONE DAY"

THE NEXT WITNESS, BASIL, AN attorney and notary, was a bespectacled, tall and upright man, and by far and away the most educated of the witnesses. He wore his hair combed back and spoke slowly and deliberately, evincing an unmistakable air of sophistication.

"George Nitsos is disrespectful and crude," he said when asked about the accused. "He doesn't even spare young schoolgirls from his vulgar humor, and he flaunts his wealth and power in the village."

Thanasis, seated with the prosecution, recalled the night of the murder. Had it not been for Basil's wise counsel, he might have taken justice into his own hands that night and gone after George.

Basil had avoided the witness stand during the first trial, but now it appeared he was determined to make amends. He spoke confidently and forthrightly.

"I was asleep when the guns were fired," he explained, "and I didn't hear them. When I went to the Gumas yard I urged Thanasis Konandreas to go and call for the doctor."

"Did Konandreas tell you that Nitsos was behind the shooting?"

"Yes. He told me in private that Nitsos had done it, and when I asked whether he thought Nitsos himself had done it, he said, 'No, he asked someone else.' Konandreas was really upset and said, 'I'm going to kill the bastard. I'm going to go home, get my pistol, and blow his brains into the air.' He was determined to kill him, and I calmed him down by telling him about his family obligations and the need to do other things at that moment. I told him to make his report when the police arrived."

"Did you speak to Nitsos at all?"

"Nitsos seemed indifferent to what was happening around him and was doing nothing to help. This combined with what Konandreas told me, made me unwilling to console him."

"You said that Nitsos was doing nothing to help when his wife was shot, and that made you wonder if he was culpable in some way. Did it not occur to you that this apathy could have been caused by shock?" the defense attorney asked.

"I don't believe so. In any case, in Kupaki we call this sort of apathy cowardice."

"Could it be that they were trying to kill Nitsos and in error they shot Panayota?"

"The killer shot the one he wanted," Basil answered, "and the fact that he shot from behind the small pear tree which was ahead of and not behind the walking couple means that he wasn't afraid of being seen."

"Did you not think that anyone else besides Nitsos could have committed the crime?"

Basil answered this at length and gave reasons why Konandreas, Vas and others were rulled out as suspects.

"My opinion is that Nitsos asked Karaiskos to kill Panayota. The entire area around the village says that the accused are guilty," he concluded.

The defense moved on to Thanasis's criminal past, bringing up the time he had beaten a man in the village.

"That incident has now been forgotten in the village," Basil said. "Today Konandreas is an exemplary family man."

"You saw Nitsos's thigh wound from the gunshot," the defense attorney said, changing directions once again. "How close was this to his genitals?"

"Perhaps about eight inches away," Basil answered. "For as good of a shooter as Socrates is, that's safe."

"What kind of man was Socrates?"

"He was a poor and good man."

"And you believe that such a good man, as you yourself call him, is capable of murder?"

"Nitsos is capable of murder and more," Basil retorted. "And he has, I'm sure, used a lot of persuasion and perhaps many threats to make Socrates commit the crime. I did say that Socrates was good, but I also said that he was poor. It was this poverty that Nitsos exploited to his advantage."

———————

Polyxeni returned home after spending a dozen days in Halkida, and my brothers and I were soon reading aloud from the last few editions of the newspaper *Ethnos*. The publication gave the details from when the defense had accused Father of being the murderer and also gave a blow-by-blow account of the examinations of Mother and several other people from the village.

Grandma Mia and Mitros wanted to know about Father's health, his state of mind, and of course, the trial.

Mother told them that this was a better court than the one in Athens. Then she answered many questions from Mitros about the jurors and added, "I just want them to get one day—just one day in jail as guilty men will do. I don't want them to come back free."

Our teacher learned that Mother was back, and during our lunch break the next day, he showed up on our front porch to ask for newspapers. "Welcome back Polyxeni," he said heartily. "How did it go?"

"Like the crab, Teacher, like the crab," Mother replied, using the Greek metaphor for a slow and difficult process.

"I think it's going in the right direction, though," the teacher said. "The judge and the prosecutor seem to have more control than they had in Athens."

Mitros appeared at his window, having heard the conversation. "The verdict comes from the jury, Teacher, not from the judge or the prosecutor!" he shouted, startling the teacher, who nearly cricked his neck turning around in bewilderment.

"I see ten years, old man," the teacher said after regaining his composure and grinning at Mitros.

"I say twenty," Mitros responded, not to be outdone.

Mother muttered under her breath as Mitros and the teacher threw numbers back and forth. "Ten years! Twenty years!" she grumbled. "All I want is just one day."

"All right, old man, you're on," the teacher said, accepting Mitros's bet. "If they get more than ten years, I will lose a hundred drachmas to you. Now what about you?"

Mitros pointed toward his favorite beehive at the end of a long row of them. "All the honey from that one in the corner."

The hive was the old man's pride and joy, which meant he was feeling awfully confident about the bet. He and the teacher had worked on it together, so the teacher, too, had to know it was a bigger honey producer.

Thanasis's sister Aggelo, who was the next witness, said that she went to the Gumases' the night of the murder, where Panayota had been taken.

Aggelo said that she heard Thanasis telling Panayota, "No, Vas didn't kill you. I told you who would.' She also recalled that next Basil told Thanasis to stop talking about killing George and getting to the telephone quickly to seek help. She also said that she heard Panayota telling Nitsos' sister, 'Now that you have devoured me...'"

"What was Nitsos doing?" the prosecution asked.

"He was silent and impassive. In fact, the entire village cried for Panayota that night except her husband."

"How were the Nitsoses getting along?" the judge asked. "Was Nitsos treating your cousin well?"

"Well? What well! He was trying to kill her for eleven years, Judge!"

The judge, after joining everybody in laughter, resumed his

questioning. "Did Panayota ever complain to you about her husband, or mention that she knew that he had plans to kill her?"

"No. Panayota loved him. Besides, I was one of the people who had told her not to marry him, so she would not have complained to me, because she would have felt that I would say, 'I told you so,' and leave her to her suffering. Of course, I would never have said nor done anything like that, but Panayota didn't know that. I did find out from others about Nitsos's plans to kill her, though. And I often told her to leave him, but she would say, 'I'm not going to let another woman take my place in this house,' and I could see how distressed she was."

"Did Panayota visit you during the afternoon the day she was killed?"

"Yes, she did."

"Did she mention anything about any plans to be at the Zakkases' later?"

"Before she left my place, she said, 'I'm going to spend a little time at the Zakkases' place.' But she didn't say, 'I'm going to the Zakkases' for dinner tonight,' as far as I can remember."

———❧———

During the recess that followed, Thanasis was surprised to see George Nitsos's family from America enter the courtroom. Reporters reached for their cameras, while onlookers buzzed with excitement.

The older Nitsos, graying at the temples and tottering unsteadily toward his son, wrapped George in a tender embrace.

But the public prosecutor, apparently unmoved by the unfolding scene, scolded the policemen standing nearby. "What are you here for?" he asked sternly. "Are you standing guard for a theater production?"

The policemen dutifully broke up the hug and then ushered George into another room, where he would spend the rest of the recess in isolation.

Effie, the next witness, said that she was next to Panayota during her last moments and heard her saying "You have devoured me."

"And even though I couldn't understand what she meant by it," Effie said, "I knew at the time that Panayota knew who was behind the shooting."

"Did you know of the relationship between Nitsos and Katina?"

Effie nodded. "I saw them kissing inside Nitsos's store only days before the murder. After the murder, I told Katina that she had made a mistake in having a relationship with an older, married man, and she replied that it was an honor that Nitsos killed his wife because of her."

The man who had the youth's party at his house on the night of the murder, was the next witness. He said he was a hunter and hunting partner of Socrates, whose gun was good enough to murder the woman. He added that they removed the feathers and ate the game right away and that what Socrates did with the bird he found suspicious.

Almost all the defense witnesses who went to the first court in Athens testified at Halkida as well and repeated prior testimonies, but the most shocking revelation came when one of them, who was recently elected president of the village council, contradicted his prior testimony. The court decided to press charges, accusing him of perjury; he ended up in custody and was later found guilty of perjury.

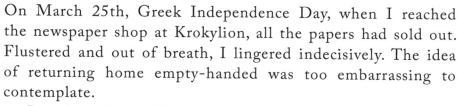

On March 25th, Greek Independence Day, when I reached the newspaper shop at Krokylion, all the papers had sold out. Flustered and out of breath, I lingered indecisively. The idea of returning home empty-handed was too embarrassing to contemplate.

Just then, Father Kritsas, the local priest, appeared like an angel. He was a close friend of Papazois, and I had served next to him as an altar boy during joint services on big holidays.

"*Father*" I said, "can you help me get a newspaper?"

Father Kritsas, standing erect and towering above me, gazed down at me bemusedly. "The shop owner has newspapers, my boy. I only have the Gospels." A smile creased his face. "Anyway, who are you?"

"I'm Lukas Konandreas, Thanasis Konandreas's son," I said quickly, "and they sent me from Kupaki for the newspaper *Ethnos*."

"Thanasis's son, eh?" Father Kritsas said, suddenly regarding me with fresh interest.

"And Papazois's nephew," I added hopefully.

"Papazois? He was at the court, wasn't he? Has he returned?"

"Yes, he's in Kupaki now."

The priest stood thinking a moment. Then he shouted to the shopkeeper in a booming voice, "How are we going to find an *Ethnos* for this boy to take to Kupaki?"

"All the papers are sold out," the shopkeeper replied.

"Stay here," Father Kritsas said. "Let me see what I can do."

The priest marched purposefully through the crowd, toward a section of the village where I knew no newspaper stores were located. A few minutes later he reappeared with a newspaper tucked under his arm.

"*Efcharisto!*", *Thank you*, I said, gratefully accepting the newspaper.

"God bless you, my son," he said and waved away my hand when I offered him the coins I'd carried with me.

Fleet of foot and light of heart, I rushed back to Kupaki, mission accomplished.

CHAPTER 28:
THINK OF YOUR CHILD

THE NEXT DAY, WHEN THE court broke for lunch, Thanasis took the public prosecutor aside and asked him if the paper about Nitsos's prior conviction has come from Athens.

"No, I'm afraid not," the prosecutor answered. "But don't worry. We don't need it just yet. I know they have it in Athens, and it will be with us when we need it."

"There's another thing," Thanasis continued.

"Yes?"

"During the trial in Athens, Nitsos claimed that he was playing a game called *"Koumkan"* at the Zakkases' on the night of the murder, didn't he?"

"Yes," the prosecutor replied after mulling over the question.

"Well, I've been thinking about it. I don't think Nitsos knows how to play that game, unless he has learned it recently in prison. He certainly never played it in Kupaki from what I remember."

"Hmm," the prosecutor said, rubbing his chin. "I see what you're getting at. It's definitely worth a try, even if it only makes the jury feel that Nitsos is a habitual liar and can't be trusted. But one thing baffles me: if Nitsos doesn't know how to play *"Koumkan"*, why didn't he name a game he knows?"

"I know how that liar's mind works," Thanasis answered. "He's too cocksure to believe he could get caught in a lie. He just had to impress the crowd. Nothing mundane will do for

George Nitsos, so if he lies about playing a game, he would lie that he played a game that sounds grand—like *"Koumkan."*

Next on the witness stand that afternoon was Socrates Karaiskos. The prosecution team managed to have George taken away to another room during Socrates's testimony, arguing that George often interrupted the witnesses and showed total contempt for court procedure. Socrates was more likely to give uninhibited testimony, the prosecution argued, if George wasn't present.

"Gentlemen of the jury," Socrates said at the first chance he got to speak, "I have been accused of killing a woman who was like a mother and a sister to me—the wife of my best man. I'm innocent. Konandreas has set me up."

"Have you and Nitsos ever gone hunting together?"

"We used to, before he injured his leg."

"Were you his confidant?"

"All the people I work for trust me and take me into their confidence."

"Were you Nitsos's protégé when he was the commander of his band?"

"No."

"Has he ever been displeased with you?"

"No."

"Have you ever argued?"

"I never get into arguments."

"On the night of the murder, Nitsos had a party. Why did he not invite you, his best man?"

"I don't move in his circles. I'm not a very important person in our community, but Nitsos is."

"Have you ever felt unable to say no to Nitsos?"

"No."

"Were you convinced, as people have testified, that in 1946 Nitsos wanted to kill his wife?"

"No," Socrates answered adamantly, "and I don't believe that story. It's a lie."

"Socrates, you've heard the witnesses. You've heard Basil.

You've heard the state police major. Why do you think Basil and the major say and believe things about you which you deny?"

"How should I know? I'm not inside Basil's head, but he's a good man, and he doesn't lie. He probably believes what he's saying because he's been misled by Konandreas. As for the major, it's his job to not completely believe things he hears during his interrogations."

"Do you think about your child, Socrates? How long has it been since you held her in your arms?"

"A whole year."

The judge sighed deeply. "Look here, Socrates," he said slowly and deliberately, "Nitsos is not here. He was sent away from the courtroom in order to let you speak freely. I'm addressing your intellect, not your emotions, so as to make you think with a cool head about your wife and your daughter. If by any chance you're involved in this murder but have promised to keep quiet, I want you to know that you're not bound by any other contract here. You stand here before Greek justice. A woman you consider equal to a mother or a sister asks for justice from her grave. So, tell the court the truth and nothing but the truth. Did anyone brainwash you to commit the murder?"

"Nobody has brainwashed me," Socrates insisted. "I have told you all I know."

"Why hadn't you eaten the partridge that you claim you shot on the day of the murder? Why did you have it ready to show as proof that your gun was used to kill the bird and not Panayota?" the public prosecutor then asked, taking over the questioning.

"I didn't have salt to cook it with," Socrates explained, "so I kept it with me until I got home."

"Then why didn't you give it to your wife to cook when you got home?"

"I forgot about it, with the news of the murder. I remembered about it only when the captain arrived later. That's why it had the feathers on it still. Besides, it didn't smell."

"You claim that you lit a fire on the hill on which you spent the night with your sheep. Did you light it as an alibi?"

"No, I did it to keep the mosquitoes off me and the jackals off my lambs."

"Can you rule out the possibility that Nitsos did it for Katina?"

"Yes, I can."

"How did Nitsos's callous conduct appear to you after the murder?"

"I wasn't there to see it. I only heard about it, and I'm not sure people are telling the truth."

"Why didn't you bring those who told you to hide your gun on that Monday morning when you were on your way to the village here to court as witnesses?"

"I didn't have the money to bring them here."

———— ✀ ————

March drew to a close, and the swallows returned to Kupaki to inspect their mud nests. The snow, meanwhile, had retreated to the surrounding mountaintops. Spring was everywhere: every bud on every tree, bush, and flower looked ready to burst.

For those in the village, however, life had come to a standstill. The village church walls had been closed since the previous autumn, when interior work had begun. And gardens remained untilled since half the villagers were away at court and the other half were insatiably gobbling up news of the trial in their spare moments.

CHAPTER 29:
"ARE YOU NOT GEORGE NITSOS"

As George Nitsos was called to the witness stand, Thanasis spotted the public prosecutor, carving his way toward him through the thick crowd of people.

"Konandreas! I have it right here!" the public prosecutor said jubilantly, tapping the inside pocket of his jacket.

A relieved Thanasis smiled back and then turned his attention to the front of the court.

After Socrates's testimony had been read in its entirety for George, he addressed the court. "I'm very saddened that I've been accused of being a wife killer," he said and went on to retell the story of how he had met and married Panayota. He then described the day of the murder and what had happened in the days that followed it. "It's all Konandreas's doing," he repeated. "He was trying to kill me, not Panayota. He had prepared the phrase 'Vas did not kill you; I told you who would.'"

"I have never denied in court anything that is true—like my relationship with Katina. Try me here as an adulterer, and I'll plead guilty. But I'm being tried as a murderer, and I plead not guilty, because I'm completely innocent of that charge. I ask you to acquit me, and I'll deliver justice the true murderers of my wife."

"If you know who the murderers are," the judge said, "why don't you name them here now?"

"Because my hands are tied. I'm behind bars, and Konandreas is free. The villagers, who fear a 'guilty' verdict, hesitate to say anything against Konandreas. If I'm convicted, they're at his mercy in Kupaki. He's a powerful man there, now that he has taken over the store and livestock and other assets that we jointly owned."

"Why did your older sister, after the card game, not go with you and your wife on the night of the murder to sleep at your place? She used to do that almost every night, didn't she?"

"She had slept at the Zakkases' three other nights before the night of the murder," George answered. "On that night, when I left with Panayota, I did ask her to come with us, but she said that she had to do her laundry the next day at the Zakkases'."

"When you were shot, were you not able to see anything? You had a flashlight, did you not? Did you not even see the shadow of the man who shot you?"

"No, I didn't."

"Did you hear the footsteps of the killer leaving?"

"No."

"Why didn't you pick your wife up from where she had fallen? Why did Gumas have to do it?"

"I was limping because of my injuries, and in my confused mental state at the time, it just didn't occur to me."

"When did your wife say, 'Vas has killed us'?"

"While she was being carried to the Gumases' house."

"What did you tell her when she said that?"

"I told her not to worry and promised her I would find the shooter."

"Why didn't you ask her if she had seen Vas?"

"I just didn't."

"I insist: why not?"

"It simply didn't occur to me to ask."

"Did your wife repeat what she had said about Vas?"

"Yes, in the Gumases' yard."

"Did you ask her this second time if she had seen him?"

"I didn't, but if I had known then that things would come to this point, I would have."

"I'm compelled to conclude from your answers that you

had no excuse not to ask your wife more about her suspicions about Vas," the judge said. "Why did you not help your wife, but instead moved away, when she was dying at the Gumases' yard?"

"Because of the trauma, I have no memory of moving away, or of Panayota being moved to the Gumases', or of the care some women gave me later, or of the moment Panayota died, or of Vas being there in the Gumases' yard."

"Did your wife know of your relationships with other women?"

"No. She trusted me. Even when that Marula woman told her that her Goddaughter had seen me and Katina kissing, Panayota did not believe it and argued for me against all the gossipmongers."

"Did you tell Katina, three hours before the murder that she should not talk even if someone took her teeth out?"

"Yes, but that had nothing to do with the murder. I meant that she shouldn't talk about our relationship. There were plenty of rumors circulating already."

The public prosecutor asked questions next.

"If you suspected Konandreas, as you have told the court earlier, why didn't you apprehend him with your suspicions? Have you spoken to him since the night of the murder?"

"No, I didn't apprehend him or speak to him after the murder," George answered, "but I did tell the police and my attorneys about my suspicions."

"Immediately after the shooting, did you think your wife was going to die, or were you hopeful about saving her life?"

"I thought she was going to live."

"Since you hoped that she would live, what did you do to save her?"

"I sent my brother-in-law Zakkas to bring a doctor."

"Why didn't you grab Konandreas and tell him, 'Thanasis, my friend, my relative, my partner'—whatever you liked to call him—'run for a doctor,' since you knew he owned a horse and Zakkas didn't?"

"I had no need for Konandreas. I sent my brother-in-law, who had more sympathy for my wife than Konandreas did."

"And what did you feel about your wife's plight?"

"I was anxious, of course. I loved her." George spoke in a reverent tone. "I still do."

"What did you do that night out of love for your wife? Did you not move away and lie down on a blanket as your wife was fighting for her life?"

"I didn't know that I was expected to act theatrically and demonstrate my love for my wife for all to see."

"Is someone who cries and brings the world down when his wife's life is in danger an actor?"

"I was taking care of my wife," George insisted, "and I had no desire to talk unnecessarily."

"When you recovered your senses at the Gumas household, did you express your intense pain to ask who had killed your wife? Would that not have been natural?"

"I was waiting for the police."

"When the police came, what did you tell them? Did you tell them, 'Vas killed her'? Those three words. Did you help them in any way to find your wife's killer?"

"I told them what my wife had said."

"From the time the gun was fired until the time your wife died from her wounds, you had nothing to say. Why were your lips sealed?"

"I told you: I was expecting the police."

"When you saw Socrates the next day, did you tell him, 'Come here, Socrates. They accuse you as the killer'?"

"No."

"Did you not say that Konandreas was once accused of being a rustler?"

"Yes, he was. A higher court later dropped the case against him."

"Why does Konandreas refer to you as *Linatsas*?"

"It's a nickname from my childhood that Konandreas spread around."

"Have you ever been found guilty in court, and if so, why?"

Thanasis, watching from the front row, tried to suppress his excitement. The prosecutor was finally going after George's record.

"Yes," George answered. "For embezzling some money from the church."

"Were you ever accused of anything during your time at Patras?"

"I can't remember. I think it was something about a broken bicycle twenty-five years ago."

"You have called Konandreas a rustler, though he was only accused and never convicted about twenty-five years ago."

"Is a bicycle incident the same as rustling, Mr. Prosecutor?"

"Mr. Nitsos, I have here a verdict that shows you were found guilty of rustling."

"I was never accused of rustling."

The prosecutor removed the papers from the inside pocket of his jacket, his eyes dancing. "I would like to submit a certified copy of the decision of the penal court of Patras, number 1703, dated May 11, 1934, along with the court records pertaining to this case."

A defense attorney rose to his feet. "Has this been submitted as part of the prosecution's records for this trial?"

"If there is an objection, I should like to hear it first," the judge said. "Then the court shall rule."

"This submission is unacceptable," the defense argued, "and against court procedure."

"The submission of documents is allowed until the end of the proceedings in any court," the prosecutor countered. "Surely the defense attorney is aware of that."

The prosecution attorneys supported the public prosecutor, and the court accepted the submission of the certificate.

Just before two p.m., the court adjourned for three hours, during which time the papers submitted by the prosecutor created a huge upheaval in the chambers.

The prosecutor winked at Thanasis on his way out of the

courtroom, and his cheerfulness was infectious. Thanasis found his own spirits lifting.

At five p.m., after the hearing resumed, the prosecutor went in for the kill.

"Nitsos," he said, making no effort to hide his exuberance, "you were accused of rustling and found guilty of stealing a lamb, were you not?"

"I don't know anything about this. This must be someone else."

"Are you not George Nitsos, son of Ioannes and Maria Nitsos, as the verdict here says?"

"No. I mean, yes, I am. But this is not about me. It must be synonymy."

"Listen, Nitsos, you have denied everything spoken against you here, and you have told us that all of the prosecution witnesses have lied. Are you now denying official papers? Now tell me how the game of *"Koumkan"* is played."

Thanasis shook his head in wonderment. The prosecutor was plying things perfectly.

"The game of what?" George asked, clearly thrown by the question.

"Koumkan". Was that not the game you said you were playing at the Zakkases' on the night of the murder?"

"Give me a deck of cards," George said, slowly regaining his usual confidence, "and I'll show you."

"Please describe the game for me in words."

"I cannot. Give me a deck, and I'll show you."

The judge, who no doubt had seen attorneys trap witnesses in numerous ways, was now staring at the public prosecutor with undisguised surprise, his mouth hanging slightly open in a most un-judgelike manner.

"Does anyone have a deck of cards?" the prosecutor's voice boomed with newfound authority. "Your Honor, I have to insist on continuing this line of questioning."

The public prosecutor then returned his attention to George.

"Nitsos, how is *"Koumkan"* played? What do the players do once the hands are dealt?"

"I'm not a card player," George said. "I've only played this game a few times, and I can't remember it now."

"Try to remember how you played it on the night of the murder. Or did you not play cards?"

"Why are you browbeating me like this?" George asked, clearly on the defensive now. "Why don't you just go ahead and make your own judgment?"

"Very well then. I will. Nitsos, you were not playing *"Koumkan"*. You were indifferent and cold, keeping the game going until eleven p.m., the time Socrates would be ready at a previously agreed upon hiding place to shoot and kill your wife."

CHAPTER 30:
NO PUNISHMENT TOO HARSH

THE PUBLIC PROSECUTOR, IN HIS closing statements told the jury that if he was asked what he would consider the greatest honor in life to be, he would answer that it was being one of them. He said that of great concern in this court was the injury inflicted on justice at the trial in Athens, where George Nitsos was portrayed as an innocent man despite all the evidence presented. When that first gunshot was fired on the defenseless, honorable, and virtuous Panayota, its echoes were heard not just among those remote mountains but all over Greece and beyond. That verdict, he continued, stirred the righteous indignation of the entire country.

"For me personally, all the evidence presented in court was unnecessary in the light of two significant sources of information: the testimony of Nitsos himself and the murder weapon.

"Nitsos was the only eyewitness to the murder," continued. "The first question for him would be this: 'Nitsos, what exactly happened at that moment? Did you hear anything? Did you see anyone?'

"No," he answered with a shrug.

"Did you think about fighting back?"

"No."

"Would you not say that this is highly suspicious? A village has been turned upside down, and all of Kupaki rushes about. His wife is carried away to safety by others. He is unconcerned. Nitsos takes no action. Oh, yes... he did ask for coffee!

"And when the injured Panayota said, 'Vas has killed us,' Konandreas intervened to say, 'Vas didn't kill you; I told you who would.' At that moment, Nitsos saw himself in front of the firing squad.

"Then all of a sudden, we hear about Nitsos's affair with Katina, who, as did Nitsos himself, admitted, on the very same night of the murder, that he told her to keep quiet, even if 'they remove your teeth' and even if 'they cut your throat.' Katina had an invitation to go to America, but Nitsos wouldn't let her go, because he was clearly infatuated with her.

"The police came and did their duty. They pursued others and determined that they were innocent. The shotguns in the village were examined, and the only gun that had been fired recently was Socrates's. The shell found at the crime scene came from his gun, so Socrates was placed under arrest as a suspect.

"The time has come for us to stop the criminal activities of a person who has had brushes with the law since his youth. Nitsos is the Rustler of Patras, the Murderer of Panayota, the man who strikes Poly and makes Katina a moral wreck.

"The ludicrous fabrications the defense has made about Konandreas—that he is a Communist, that he conspired with the Communist Party of Greece to kill Nitsos, that on the night of the crime, he missed Nitsos and killed his own cousin Panayota—are more examples of Nitsos's desperate attempts to evade justice.

"In addition to his remarks about Konandreas, Nitsos lashed out against government employees, policemen, and anyone else who tried to find the truth. That confirmed his culpability.

"We don't wish for Nitsos's destruction. We have no reason to be vengeful. For us, Nitsos is a Greek citizen who should be protected by Greek laws until proven guilty. And guilty he has been proven now."

The prosecutor finished his closing argument by advising the jury to ignore anything that the defense called "extenuating circumstances." This, Thanasis knew, meant he was suggesting that no punishment—not even the death penalty—would be too harsh for George and Socrates.

After the public prosecutor, the attorneys on the prosecution team painted George Nitsos as a repeat offender, as a womanizer who had treated his wife with unusual cruelty and contempt, and as a coward, a man who for years had relied on his charm and political clout to get his way. He was in love with Katina, a woman he had prevented from going to America, had warned to remain silent about their affair, and had promised to marry as soon as he was out of jail.

As for the murder itself, it had clearly been premeditated, with George arranging things to make sure that he—and he alone—was with Panayota as they walked a narrow and treacherous footpath in the dark.

The prosecution attorneys added that Socrates could not be accounted for between the hours of eight-thirty p.m. and one a.m. His decision to call out to a fellow shepherd in the wee hours of the morning looked, in retrospect, like a transparent attempt to establish his presence on the hills outside of the village. Likewise, the dead partridge, unplucked and uneaten, only cast more suspicion on him. If his gun was all but unusable, how had he managed to kill the bird?

The prosecution attorneys finally presented a letter written by George's father in response to a letter from Skevi after the murder:

I'm curious to know why you make all these complaints to me when you know that I have no responsibility whatsoever in this business. I left George as an eight-year-old, and when he grew up, you made him your son-in-law by force. You lived around him for the past fourteen years, and now you tell me about my "prodigal son." Were you not there to see what was going on?

If, as you say, my son is such a good-for-nothing, why didn't you tell your daughter: "My child, this is no life for you. Leave that awful man. We can do without all this luxury. Let us go back to our home and eat our vegetables together?"

But you did not. And now, after fourteen years, you tell me that my son is no good. I sent them a letter some years back, asking them to get a divorce since they could not live peacefully together. And do you know what they both answered? They wrote, 'We're doing very well together. People say those things because they are jealous.'

Now that you have killed Panayota and got my son into jail, you write to tell me that you didn't see what was coming and that my son is a murderer. You are the murderer. You have killed your own daughter.

You have locked us out of our own house, as well, just when we were planning to visit our relatives there. I don't know what you hope to achieve with all this, but I hope it makes you feel lighter in your heart.

Now your destiny is to cry like the partridge, because you, too, were only able to see so far and no further.

With sympathy from all of us,
Ioannes Nitsos

CHAPTER 31:
THE BEST DEFENSE

"GEORGE NITSOS IS A HERO," the defense attorney proclaimed, pausing to read the reactions of the onlookers to the opening line of his closing argument for the defense.

"George Nitsos is a hero," he repeated. "He was in the forefront of the war against the Communists. As the commander of the band in his district, he fought for the liberties we have today. If a man like him, a man of the mountains, unchecked and free, had never shown any propensity for cruelty and had never committed arbitrary acts of violence, why would he suddenly develop such a propensity?

"Nitsos was held in very high esteem in Kupaki. He was the elected village council president, a post that is constantly under public scrutiny. In order to tarnish this image and make him look like a common criminal, the prosecutor looked desperately for something in Nitsos's past and gleefully discovered an old conviction from his youth—a conviction for rustling that is totally unrelated to this case.

"The accusation that Nitsos showed a strange inertia after the crime and did not chase the killer is ill-considered. Had he staged the whole incident, as the prosecution argues, he would have put on a show of heroism and pursued the gunman. It's precisely because he didn't organize the shooting that he behaved like a normal man in a crisis, a man whose wife was fatally wounded, a man that trauma had rendered inactive. He was not guilty of the murder, and therefore he didn't think it necessary to deflect suspicion from himself. And that's exactly why it didn't strike him that he ought to exploit the advantage his wife gave him by saying, 'Vas has killed us.'

"As for Socrates, the entire prosecution team couldn't succeed in burying the fact that he has never in his life done anything remotely criminal. An orphan, he overcame his vulnerable social position by hard work and determination. Why would such a caring family man suddenly get it into his head to throw all this away and turn into a killer for a few drachmas?"

"The prosecution claims that the shell found at the crime scene came from Socrates's shotgun," the defense attorney continued. How could men with the military experience of Nitsos and Karaiskos not have found ways to destroy or dispose of such revealing evidence? The police captain discovered this much celebrated shell a full twelve hours after the crime, after the entire village of Kupaki had trampled over the crime scene. Anyone wishing to incriminate Nitsos and Karaiskos could easily have planted the shell there. The shell was not sent for fingerprinting. Instead, the captain carried it from house to house, leaving it on the investigation desks, to which Konandreas, who had become his shadow by now, had unchecked access.

"The shell sent to the forensic laboratory as evidence was not the shell found at the crime scene. This is a very crucial point. I cannot stress it enough. If it cannot be proven beyond doubt that a certain shell was actually found at the murder scene, then it follows that the gun it was fired from cannot be proven beyond doubt to be the murder weapon, therefore the owner of the gun cannot be accused of murder.

"The way the police captain conducted his investigation in Kupaki leaves much to be desired. He slept in Vas's house on the day he arrived there. Did he not think for a moment that he would be compromising the investigation by accepting the hospitality of a suspect? Surely, he had heard by then that Panayota had named Vas before she died.

"Our well-known forensic expert has told you in the presence of other forensic experts that from six yards away—the distance the round was supposed to have been fired from—and on a terrain with a gradient of thirty-five degrees, which exactly describes the murder scene, Socrates's shotgun would have made a wound of more than twenty-two centimeters in diameter. The abdominal wounds which Panayota Nitsos succumbed to were only fourteen centimeters in diameter.

"Nitsos was injured by three bullets hitting different parts of his body. If one of them had hit him in the carotid artery or penetrated his abdomen and the peritoneum, he would have died with Panayota. Some of Nitsos's wounds were not very far away from these parts. Why would Nitsos take such a risk, trusting the marksmanship of the gunman he had allegedly hired, to prove that he is innocent? If Nitsos had died, would anyone have dared accuse him? And we know now how close he was to dying."

"Panayota lived for more than half an hour after being shot," he continued, "If Nitsos had organized the shooting, would he have let her live that long? Would he not have worried whether she had recognized Socrates in the light of the flash from the gun when it was fired at her? Would he not have stopped her from revealing any information to the villagers who had come to help her if he thought that this information could be potentially damaging to him? If Nitsos was the organizer of the crime, why would he be content with an injured Panayota when he could have had a dead Panayota by the time the villagers arrived? All he had to do was to tell Socrates, if Socrates had indeed done the shooting at his behest, to finish Panayota off.

"To get our answers, let us turn our attention away from Nitsos and Karaiskos and focus it on Konandreas, a man who stands to gain huge benefits if Nitsos is convicted."

"Sole proprietorship of the store in the village center," the attorney said, still hammering away. "Sole ownership of livestock hitherto jointly owned, the presidency of the village council—the list is long. After Nitsos was taken out of the picture, Konandreas became the uncrowned king of Kupaki and the area around it. But Greek justice will not let him deceive her. He will not only have to account for the crime of murdering Panayota, but also for that of looting George Nitsos's wealth. After the trial of Nitsos versus the people of Greece, you may well see the trial of Konandreas versus Nitsos and Konandreas versus the people of Greece.

"Let us now move on to Vas. The phrase, 'Vas has killed us,' that was uttered by the victim has not been properly understood by the unqualified people who took over this case. The interrogators asked the wrong questions. With the clarity of vision—and this has been scientifically proven—that comes to people in a crisis, Panayota had put two and two together, seen the whole plot, and realized who her murderer was, but it was too late to be of any help to her.

"The most tangible proof of Nitsos' innocence is not his own conduct after the murder but the conduct of Konandreas. He presents himself as already possessing the knowledge that Nitsos would be the killer, yet he had been silent for years until the murder. And his witnesses testify that he told the dying victim, 'Vas didn't kill you; I told you who would.' What a heartless thing to say to a dying woman! The question we all have to ask is not why Nitsos showed inertia during a life-threatening crisis, but why Konandreas showed inertia for so many years when he knew, in his own words, who would kill Panayota.

"If it were not for Katina, suspicion would have been focused relentlessly on Konandreas. The murder scene is located between his house and the house of his mother-in-law, Aliki Gumas. He passed the spot only fifteen minutes before the first shot at eleven p.m. In fact, he walked barely five feet away from where the killer would place himself to shoot at Panayota. Could he have cold-bloodedly set up the scene for the murder before going home to his wife and children? At the precise moment of the crime, his wife was on the balcony of his house and his mother-in-law at the window of her house. Were they waiting for something?

"The letter from Nitsos's father to Panayota's mother that was triumphantly read aloud here by the prosecution does not reveal the fissures in the relationship between George Nitsos and Panayota Nitsos, as the prosecution would have us believe. It reveals the burning envy of a section of the villagers of Kupaki—the envy that continues to manifest itself in the baseless allegations against Socrates and George Nitsos that you have listened to here.

"The mistake made in Athens was not the jury's decision to acquit the accused, but the court's decision to call the jury's verdict *peplanimeni*—in other words, a judicial error!

"Gentlemen of the jury! Nitsos and Karaiskos are not here before you as guilty men, but as innocent citizens of Greece whose rights you have a duty to protect. A verdict for their acquittal has been issued from a court similar to this one. The disgruntled prosecution called those Athenian jurors incapable. They now praise you and flatter you with the same cynicism. They feel they can make you pass the verdict they want you to pass by fooling you into believing that you will be seen as the 'clean jury' from the real Greece, the great town of Halkida, as opposed to the 'corrupt jury' in the corrupt capital. They think that you're vain enough to say, 'We're better, and we're going to prove our superiority with a decision that will be diametrically opposed to that of the Athenian jury, a decision that will be popular with many people and segments of the press.'

"Gentlemen of the jury! The opinion of the judges, who have also complimented you here in court, is insignificant. That's why the legislators determined that you, the people, are going to decide, and not the judges. Because you decide as free citizens of Greece, whereas they decide as officials of the legal system.

"Countless innocent lives, victims of judicial errors, have been destroyed ever since the start of our legal system because of officials seeing no further than the letter of the law. You have the choice to look beyond books and see the human side of justice. You have the choice to be the kind face of Greek justice that emphasizes the protection of the innocent. You have the choice not to be the harsh mask of the law that has to make an example by punishing—and often punishing the weak and the innocent in its zeal.

"The defense team joins me in imploring you not to wash your hands of your moral duty like Pontius Pilate. Our constitution and our laws protect the personal freedoms of the Greek citizens by having juries deciding the outcome of important trials.

"Gentlemen of the jury," the defense attorney dropped his voice to an audible whisper. "You're answerable only before God, for He is the voice of your honor and your conscience."

Each member of the defense team did address the jury at length and all went fairly smoothly until the leading defense attorney, who Thanasis had always considered the foremost attorney on the defense's team, if not in all of Greece, stood to make his closing remarks. He accused the prosecutor of meeting and conversing with the police major outside the court and of making scornful reference to the jurors from the court in Athens as bank employees without legal knowledge. He then characterized the public prosecutor as "a glorious orator, but with little evidence or logic to complement his oratory excesses, which are a study in verbal acrobatics—exactly what one would expect from someone who's in love with himself and suffers from autism."

The public prosecutor stood. "Permission to speak, Your Honor."

"Granted."

"I'd like to have these malignant words, which incidentally best describe this attorney's client, who he seems desperate to save from a just conviction, added to the court records."

The leading attorney continued and said that someone unknown to him was following him daily and that he had complained to the public prosecutor about it. Next, he began reading from a book about fingerprints. He then pivoted to Goethe, the famous German poet, who he said had not cried when his child had died, just as George Nitsos had not shed a tear for Panayota in her final hour. And soon he was reciting Greek romantic poetry as he described the "true love" between

George and Panayota. By the time he finished his oratory, he had, while wiping away a tear, eulogized his own dead parents, who had left behind three orphaned girls.

While the attorney's performance impressed at least one teary-eyed juror, it fell flat with the judge when he announced he would do whatever he could to avoid ever appearing in another case presided over by the present judge.

The judge, who had by now already begun disciplinary action against this attorney responded by calling his comments inappropriate. "I'm going to report you to the Bar of Halkida," he said icily.

He then addressed the rest of the court. "With the patently false accusations that the defense attorney has leveled against most of us here, his own profile appears more and more like that of his client, who is aptly called Linatsas."

Was the leading attorney delusional, Thanasis wondered, or was it a strategy by the clever attorney to influence the jurors by whatever means possible, given that a juror, who Thanasis knew was a retired military officer apparently toughened by his career, cried along with him?

———————— ❧ ————————

"Lukas," Polyxeni said to me one afternoon when she could no longer take the constant nagging from Mitros and Papazois, "go fetch us a newspaper. Otherwise these two will give me no peace."

"If you see Father Kritsas," Papazois said, "remember to thank him again for the newspaper the other day."

I nodded and hurried off to Krokylion, where another large crowd had gathered in the café to wait for the newspaper bus. While I was waiting for the bus, others who were waiting made some comments supporting Nitsos and Karaiskos and against my father. They were very upsetting.

As soon as the papers arrived, I bought one and raced to Kupaki. The tears I had kept in check poured freely down my cheeks.

Not long after turning onto the cobblestone path toward the village, I caught sight of a tall man plowing a field with two mules. He was holding a whip in one hand and gripping the handle of a plow with the other. An older woman, most likely his wife, was following him and spreading seeds in the furrows. It was Father Kritsas, with his vestment pulled up and tied to his back. His priest's hat was nowhere in sight.

"*Father,*" I hollered as the mules turned to make another run in the opposite direction.

"Yes?" He pulled hard, lifting the entire plow in the air and turning it so he could face me. "Oh, it's you again!" he said, panting from the exertion.

"Papazois told me to thank you for the *Ethnos* you gave me to give to him the other day," I said.

With rivulets of sweat running down his face and into his beard and the hair on his chest, Father Kritsas reached over the fence and enveloped the back of my head with his huge hands, holding them there.

I made no effort to escape. I felt comforted by the old man's touch.

"Your father is good," he said. "He has them this time."

The fears I had felt just minutes earlier at the café evaporated in the gentle spring breeze.

CHAPTER 32:
MESSAGE FROM DARKNESS
– DARKNESS OVERCOME?

THE LAST OF THE CLOSING arguments were finished by 11 p.m. the day before decision day at which point Thanasis left the court with his sister Aggelo and Aunt Skevi.

When they reached the seafront, they found the streets silent, save for the waves of the straits breaking gently on the shore. The early spring air was mild, and the only illumination besides the moonlight came from the lamp posts along the promenade. Thanasis, as he watched the light play on the crests of the waves, thought he could go on forever watching the light reflections. The sea had always fascinated him. Was it because he hailed from the mountains? All he knew for sure was he could unwind now, safe in the knowledge that he had done all he could do for Panayota. He let the moonlight drive his worries away. The case was beyond his control now and would be decided by the jury.

A majestic castle stood guard over the town, towering atop the hill across the straits, and Thanasis couldn't help fancying that it, too, was affected by all this serenity, but soon he could feel the familiar anxieties edging their way into his mind. He walked toward their hotel with a sigh. It had been good while it lasted.

The three slept in the same room together and were soon sound asleep, their fatigue having stolen every last ounce of energy.

The next morning, Thanasis awoke to sunlight on his face as the sun crested the hill in the east. He needed coffee. He rose to get himself a strong cupful, making special pains not to wake the others.

Aggelo stirred in the bed. She was smiling at him. "Let me tell you about the dream I had," she said before he could ask her if she wanted coffee. "Let me tell you who came to me in my dream."

Aunt Skevi grunted, having been so rudely jarred from her sleep.

"Your late husband, of course," Thanasis replied.

"No" Aggelo said. "It was Panayota."

"Oh?" Thanasis didn't know what else to say.

"And they will be convicted."

"I'm sure it will come true," Thanasis said, unable to resist mocking his sister.

"This was different," Aggelo insisted. "It was so real. She was very clear about the conviction."

"Oh... oh... my child!" Aunt Skevi obviously didn't share Thanasis's cynicism. "Was she all right, Aggelo?"

"It was at our field in outside the village," Aggelo said and began to narrate her dream to her captive audience of two. "She was opposite, standing in the neighbors' field. She called across to me. 'Aggelo! Aggelo!' And I responded. I asked her where she'd been."

By now, Skevi was crying. "Where had she been? Oh, where?"

"She wouldn't tell me, Aunt. Are you going to let me finish?"

Skevi blew her nose and waited in silence for Aggelo to finish the story.

The crux of the narration was that Panayota and the "others"—whoever they were—were "preparing" for Linatsas. They had made all necessary "arrangements" to "take care" of him.

Thanasis wasn't sure how the phrase was meant to be interpreted. "Was Panayota saying she'd take care of George in the hereafter the way she did during their marriage?" he asked his sister. "Or was she implying they would make him pay for all the suffering he caused her?"

"I don't know, Brother," Aggelo answered. "I'm just repeating exactly what she said."

Thanasis had never considered himself superstitious and therefore treated Aggelo's dream like a joke. However, he had to admit that he found comfort in a message from the other world predicting George's conviction. That said, he was unwilling to leave anything to chance.

"Find a seat in the front row," he advised his aunt later that morning. "Directly opposite the jury bench. And do stare at the jurors constantly. Make eye contact. Make it difficult for them to avoid your eyes. Make sure they see Panayota in them."

The foreman of the jury stepped forward. He and his fellow jury members had been deliberating since half past ten in the evening. Now, two and a half hours later, the crowd that had filled the courtroom beyond capacity and spilled out into the grounds was stirring impatiently. Thanasis, surveying the whole scene from his front-row seat, realized that everyone on hand, even the latecomers behind him jostling for a better view, was waiting for closure.

"With honor and conscience," the foreman began, "a verdict has been reached by the majority of the jury."

The courtroom fell silent as those in the crowd leaned forward and strained to hear the foreman's words.

"Both of the accused, George Nitsos and Socrates Karaiskos, have been found guilty. While their mental state at the time can't be called insanity, their capacity to fully understand the injustice of their actions was considerably diminished..."

The foreman's words were lost in the cheerings of the crowd, though some grumbles and protests could also be heard. Despite the noise from the crowd, Thanasis could make out the gist of the jury's decision. George was sentenced to twenty years in jail. Socrates earned eighteen years and one month, the latter being for his illegal use of a firearm. Both were to lose their political rights for a period of ten years, during which time they would not be allowed to vote from prison. They were also to pay the court expenses jointly. Finally, the court ruled that they were to pay Skevi, ten thousand drachmas for the mental agony their actions had brought upon her.

"You have five days to appeal against this decision," the judge said, addressing the two defendants.

"The defense fully intends to appeal against this unjust decision," the leading defense attorney answered.

A vindicated Aggelo, who along with Skevi was seated beside Thanasis, turned to him. "See, Brother," she said. "You mocked me when I said that Panayota came to me in my dreams and told me about the verdict."

Skevi, silent until now, spoke. "That man from the jury said that they were guilty. If they know those bastards killed my daughter, why aren't they being shot dead?"

A defense attorney from Halkida, called to Thanasis across the court. "Are you happy with the verdict this time, Mr. Konandreas?"

"Counsel," Thanasis hollered back, "pleased I am, but satisfied I'm not. They'll go to jail for a few years and will be among us again one day. Panayota can never be with us again. They should pay for their crime and suffer the same way my cousin did."

One of the jurors, approached Thanasis. "That's what I would have liked, too," he said.

In fact, as Thanasis learned a short while later from his local attorney, a few jurors had proposed even the death sentence, but the majority had vetoed it.

It was late, nearly three o'clock in the morning, when Thanasis, Aggelo, and Aunt Skevi were walking on the seafront towards their hotel.

Aggelo's noticed the full moon cutting through the overcast skies and brightening the cityscape and her mind travelled to the night of the murder, when there was no moon at all. She pointed her finger at the full moon, "Where were you the night poor Panayota was shot, and I was running to the Gumas house nearly killing myself in the darkness?"

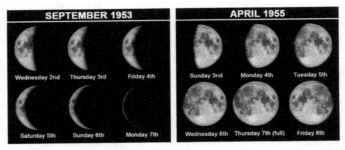

Photo on left: Moon on the night of the murder, September 6-7, 1953.
Photo on right: Moon on decision night, April 7-8. 1955.

CHAPTER 33:
THE TELEGRAM

THE CHURCH BELLS RANG THAT morning at eight o'clock, signaling the students to assemble in front of the school in Kupaki. After a brief prayer, we queued up for breakfast, which had been prepared by one of the mothers.

The sun was already warming the air, and I felt cheerful as I stood in line to have my cup filled. Ahead of me, steam rose from a huge vat, whose contents, a mixture of water, powdered milk, and sugar, simmered over a steady burning fire.

Just as I neared the front of the line, my great-uncle's voice boomed from the direction of our house. That was nothing new. Mitros often cursed his wife or shouted at the goat.

I had barely begun to drink my milk when Polyxeni appeared on the path, walking briskly toward the school. I hurried to meet her, as did my brothers and our teacher.

"What news, Polyxeni?" the teacher asked. "Anything from Halkida yet?"

"Yes!" Mother called out cheerfully. "Thanasis sent me this telegram," she said and waved the piece of paper in the air like a flag. "Guilty! They've been convicted. They'll be sent to prison."

I felt an overwhelming urge to scream and shout but resisted.

"Good, good!" the teacher said in a jubilant voice. Then his smile faded. "Is that why Mitros was screaming a while ago from his house? Did he beat me on the bet?"

"I'm afraid he did, teacher. The big guy got twenty years, and the sidekick eighteen."

"Oh no!" the teacher lamented, sounding more pleased than someone who had just lost a bet should. "Please tell Mitros I'll pass that way to see him, will you?"

As we continued with our meal, some of the students began making quick calculations.

"I'll be thirty years old when they come out," one said.

"I'll have a wife and two sons," said another.

"Too bad they didn't get the firing squad."

Although overjoyed by the news, I felt another emotion, one I hadn't anticipated: sympathy. I hadn't shown it during the trial, but now I worried on behalf of the students whose families had supported George and Socrates.

That afternoon, when I arrived home from school, everybody appeared content, but there were no loud cheers of celebration.

The teacher arrived next door a few minutes later to visit Mitros and admit defeat. "Congratulations, old man," he said and produced a hundred-drachma bill from his pocket. "Here's the money I owe you."

Mitros, despite looking ill, appeared happy about the outcome of the trial. "Don't worry about the money," he said, waving away the bill. He gestured toward his hives. "You've given me more help and encouragement with those babies than a hundred drachmas can buy."

It was the Friday before Palm Sunday, and Mother had us children in church that evening. After services, although everyone knew about the court's decision, no one openly spoke about it. Most seemed quietly content with the verdict, and only a handful approached Polyxeni to quietly whisper their satisfaction. The less said about the matter, most seemed to think, the better for everyone.

PART V:
LIFE AFTER THE COURTS

Holy Week arrived. Father was home after over a month's absence at Halkida, and along with fasting and joining the family for church services nearly every day, he was assessing his financial troubles. He was very thankful that his attorneys had reduced their fee to a mere fraction of what was customary at the time. It was an act of generosity, Thanasis thought, disproving the commonly held notion that lawyers were heartless. That had certainly helped, but he knew he was penniless.

I was at the store one day that week helping my father when two prosecution witnesses who had spent their own money at Halkida came to the store. Thanasis asked me to pay them with money from the store's counter. To his great embarrassment, there was not enough cash in the counter or his pocket to pay both of them back. He was forced to ask one to wait a few days.

"I can't believe this has happened to us," my father said softly after the men had left. "I have never been left without money my entire life. I've always had some, even when I was a young shepherd. And now this has happened to me."

Thanasis was certainly a tightfisted trader with sound business instincts and a head for arithmetic. He could impress customers, many of them far better educated than him, by working out percentages in his mind and offering them deals while they were still calculating. Perhaps because of his aptitude for math, he knew better than anyone the long odds he was facing regarding his children's education.

His children would have to move to a larger town for high school and pay for room and board. As for a university education, that was something only the rich in Greece could entertain. How would Thanasis possibly save enough money in such a short time to put his four children through school?

"When we had the means," his wife lamented one night, "we threw them into the straits of Halkida. I knew this was coming, but I couldn't stop it."

"I couldn't stop it, either," Thanasis responded. "But my children will go to university. God will help us find a way."

Determined not to let go his dream, even if he knew little of what it would take financially or if his children were even capable of pursuing a university education, he devised a long and arduous work schedule for the entire family. The children, besides being responsible for their schoolwork, worked sixteen-hour days that included laboring in the fields, doing household chores, helping with the bee-keeping, collecting milk from the family's shepherds, making cheese, and manning the village store.

George's older sister, returned to Kupaki just before summer, and my friends and I watched as the shutters of the Nitsos house were opened for the first time in nearly two years. It was rumored that George's parents would be staying there.

Along with the opening of Nitsos's house came a demand by Skevi, the mother of Panayota, that her daughter's dowry be returned. In a village where dowries only travelled in one direction—from the house of the bride to the house of the groom—this silent, desolate return of a dowry to the murdered woman's home was no small event.

We watched in stunned silence, several of the villagers crossing themselves in disbelief, as Panayota's dowry was marched back to the home of her mother. This was not the dowry of a rosy-cheeked village maid, but that of a murdered middle-aged woman. There was no suntanned, rough-handed, broad-shouldered groom dancing to clarinet music, leaping from boulder to boulder on the village path with the freedom of reckless youth. The dowry wasn't going to the groom's house, with his parents and siblings welcoming it, but to the old house of a buried bride, its only inhabitant a grieving old woman. Instead of the happy music of the clarinet, the wails of Skevi filled our ears.

A few days later, as the summer vacation drew near, my older brother and I climbed a pair of cherry trees after lunch at St. Anthony Cemetery and started filling ourselves with the delicious ripe fruit. We had only been there a few minutes when we caught sight of the diminutive figure of Skevi, Panayota's mother, who was holding a small sickle and a towel at the cemetery gate. She had come to clear her daughter's grave of the dry wild grass covering it and light a candle. Soon she was crying and talking to her daughter as she stood over the grave.

My brother and I, no longer able to enjoy our feast, slid down from the trees, accidentally startling Skevi, who crossed herself fearfully.

"Aunt Skevi," I said after we climbed the lawn terraces and reached the path that led to the gate, "why have you got 'Panayota Soulias' instead of 'Panayota Nitsos' on the cross?"

"That was my daughter's name, my golden boy," she replied, her voice catching as she sobbed.

"Wasn't she Panayota Nitsos?" I persisted.

"No, no, my little one. She never was. She was always a Soulias."

My brother spoke up. "But the papers were calling her Nitsos."

"I don't know about the papers, but I'll never let her have that bastard's name in the other world. Never!" Skevi studied us a moment. "Have your parents never told you how bad it is to eat cherries from cemetery trees?"

"No," I said, my mind struggling to make a connection between this and Panayota's last name. "Why?"

Skevi responded by lecturing us on how bad it was to eat

cherries from trees growing inside the cemetery, which, as she put it, "belonged to the dead."

I tried to counter with what I knew of gardening, citing various facts learned in school, but she turned a deaf ear to my comments.

"Did you eat the cherry pits, too?" Skevi asked.

The question unnerved me. "A few," I answered nervously. "At the beginning, when we first got here and ate quickly, we swallowed a few."

My brother nodded gravely.

"Oh ... no ... my children!" Skevi shook her head and clicked her tongue. "Those are the bones of the dead, and you have swallowed them?"

A wave of nausea washed over me. Without another word, I hurried home, leaving my brother behind. I bit down the fear and disgust that threatened to overpower me as I ran, managing to keep the cherries down all the way back. Once I reached home, I vacated the cherrie, and I felt like my insides were being shoveled out, much like the dirt mixed with bones that had been flung from Socrates's spade when he had dug Panayota's grave the day after the murder.

It took a lot of reassurance from my parents and grandmother to put my mind at rest.

The village began to heal that summer of 1955. The prosecution witnesses used the words perjurer and corrupt less and less when referring to the defense witnesses, who, since George and Socrates's conviction, had been bending over backward to treat the prosecution witnesses respectfully. Thanasis seemed to be letting go, too.

We were finishing dinner around the fireplace one evening that autumn when George's brother and sister knocked at out door and asked permission to visit. My parents invited them inside and offered them seats near the fireplace.

Alex, George's brother, who had returned from America earlier that year, had driven into the village in his brand-new purple Lincoln with a white top, the wide-eyed villagers looking on in amazement. I had never expected him to come to our house. My parents, too, looked utterly surprised.

"Time for bed," Father said.

My siblings and I, who had been sitting beside the fire and pretending not to be sleepy, reluctantly shuffled off for bed. This was one adult conversation we wouldn't be allowed to hear.

As Alex and his sister took a couple of the places we children had left the room, Thanasis reflected on the similarities between George and his brother. Funny, talented with a guitar in his hands or a vocal melody on his lips—Alex was just as entertaining as his jailed brother, but he had something George did not: sincerity. He was also less vulgar. Even the most puritanical members of the community had no reason to think harshly of Alex Nitsos.

Alex was direct. "We decided to visit you at night," he said, "because we didn't want people to see us."

"We want to put this thing behind us and build bridges," his sister said in an apologetic tone that took Thanasis off guard. "If we've done anything unforgivable toward you, we're truly sorry."

Polyxeni excused herself and returned a few minutes later with a tray stacked with homemade bread, feta cheese, walnuts, chestnuts, and grilled herring. She also brought homemade wine.

"Perhaps too late," Alex said, "but we know the truth now."

"Panayota was the best wife any man could have," the sister added, her eyes moist with tears. "But George is our brother, and there was nothing else we could think of at the time but to believe in his innocence and support him. We had no choice. No other option even entered our minds at the time."

Did she believe her brother was a wife-killer? It seemed to Thanasis that she was coming awfully close to admitting such a thing.

As the night progressed, Alex drank glass after glass of the homemade wine, which loosened his tongue.

"Do you know, Thanasis," he began, his words slightly slurred, "I was the one who urged Panayota to be brave and do something to break up the relationship between Poly and George. And she took my advice." He paused for another sip of wine and then hiccupped. "She intercepted that letter he had sent to that girl and read it aloud in the village square. Hats off to her. It wasn't timidity that made her stay with George; it was love. And my brother didn't deserve it. No, he didn't deserve it.

"We were *this* close," Alex continued, trying to focus his eyes on the thumb and index finger of his left hand. "We were this close to using our contacts to persuade, perhaps even buy that juror in Athens who wouldn't go with the rest of the jury. That would have put an end to it all, and there would have been no grounds for the case to be sent to Halkida."

Thanasis knew now that the only juror in Athens to dissent in the case was an independent and honorable man but was not sure if he had ever been approached by his side. "Well," he said, "good for you that you didn't get any closer. If that juror was who I think he was, he would have been too honorable to be for sale, and you would now be behind bars with your brother."

Thanasis had no doubt that it wasn't the drink talking; Alex was telling them the truth. In fact, later that year, a cousin of George's would actually name the figure that they'd been prepared to offer the juror: twenty thousand drachmas.

"She," Alex continued pointing at his sister, "and I are now planning to sell our houses in the city. There's no other way we'll be able to afford the legal fees for both trials."

"Tell me about it," Thanasis said dryly.

"He's left me a poor man," Alex said. "My brother has left me a poor man, Thanasis."

Thanasis couldn't help thinking that the poverty of Alex Nitsos, living in Michigan and driving from Athens in his purple and white Lincoln convertible, was quite different from his own.

He noticed the skies brightening outside. It was almost dawn.

"If he left you a poor man, Alex" he said, laughing bitterly, "I'll need to find another word for what he has turned me into." He nodded to the tray Polyxeni had brought out hours earlier. "Have some of that herring. It was grilled right here at this fireplace."

"You murderer!" a woman screamed. "You dare come back here? Get lost, you... you son of the devil! Why didn't you go to hell, never to return?"

By now many of the shuttered windows in Kupaki had been hurriedly thrown open. Heads poked forth to see what all the fuss was about. I joined a handful of men who rushed to the village square, where four paths met, and where Papadia, Papazois's wife, was giving Socrates an earful.

It was September1962. More than seven years had passed since the trial in Halkida. Socrates, having had his jail time reduced in exchange for his labor and good behavior, was back. Until now, he had managed to keep a low profile by avoiding the store and walking the paths only sparingly. This afternoon, he had apparently crossed paths with Papadia, who had refused to give him a wide berth. It was here, nearly two decades earlier, that Panayota had read aloud George's love letter to Poly, where George and Socrates had organized their wild revelry, complete with a donkey dressed in human clothes.

Socrates, rather than return Papadia's fire, uttered not a single word. Instead, he doubled his pace and strode quickly toward his home, where his wife, who also had heard the commotion, had come running out. She grabbed him when he reached the yard and pulled him inside.

For my part, I was now in my late teens. I'd just returned to the village from Athens, where we had lived since 1958. Having just taken the entrance test for the Medical School of the University of Athens, I was enjoying a brief vacation in Kupaki. A couple of weeks later, the news that I had passed the entrance test reached me, and I forgot all about Socrates's clash with Papadia. After my name was printed in the major

221

Athenian dailies, which published all the names of the students who had gained admission to the various prestigious faculties of the university, congratulatory messages poured in from all directions from friends and relatives, close and distant.

But my celebratory mood vanished when I realized that I didn't have the money needed for books and tuition. My only hope was to find a job, but those, too, were hard to come by in the 1960s in Greece.

Fortunately, through the kindness of acquaintances, I found paid employment just before the academic year was to start. Despite having a job, I still had no tuition money for the first semester. How would I pay?

Just as I was running out of options, the right-wing government passed a law that made tuition for a university education free. The Communist Party of Greece had been asking for just such a law for several years, claiming that the Soviets enjoyed a free education.

The Communists had been taking to the streets since early spring, chanting the slogan, "Free Paedia, no dowry for Sofia." Princess Sofia was the daughter of King Pavlos and Queen Frederica of Greece. Her marriage with King Carlos of Spain was being subsidized with substantial money from the Greek government. The money was called a present, but to the populace it was a dowry. Then there was the center coalition, led by George Papandreou, who was competing with the Communists for the Socialists' vote and who was promising the nation that, if elected, he would provide "free Paedia." With the freedom we enjoyed, he claimed, we would be "better off than the Soviets."

Now there was no need of tuition. Little did my late grandfather "Dowry Konandreas" know that, years after he had failed to get a good dowry for his son, his grandchild and the Queen of Spain would get from the same source a very good dowry indeed.

Later, I stumbled upon an enterprising way to pay for the additional expenses of medical school: I took notes at lectures, organized them, and typed them up, and they became quick reference texts sold to other students. I had my own money, a Volkswagen, and a small savings account, the latter of which I would one day use to pay for my transatlantic move. The future, precarious one moment, was suddenly smiling on me.

At sunset one sultry evening during a trip to Greece in 2005, I decided to light candles on the graves of departed loved ones at the St. Anthony's Cemetery outside the village.

The cherry trees, the fruit of which caused decades earlier such fear and nausea, were long gone. Only dry grass and a stately row of cypresses remained to soften the imposing sea of marble tombs, the lonely chapel, and the enclosing stone wall. I could just make out the sound of children playing soccer in the village, their laughter interrupted every now and then by the candles crackling on the gravestones. A lizard scurried swiftly past. To the east loomed the top of St. Nicholas Hill. To the north, a smattering of red clay-tiled village rooftops could be seen in and amongst the trees.

As I stood over my father Thanasis's grave, I noticed a fascinating symmetry. Nine paces to his left was the grave of George Nitsos. Situated nine paces to the right was the grave of Panayota. Although the positioning was likely coincidental, it got me in a contemplative mood. What was Thanasis doing between them? Was he protecting Panayota from George? Was he keeping them apart as he had not done in 1935?

Had he done the latter, Panayota might have been free to marry a man worthy of her values. Her work ethic, her spirit, and her keen mind would have had a chance to flourish in the deep, nurturing soil of our village.

On the walk back towards my childhood home, I thought about how the community and culture had evolved since the days of the events with my father and Panayota in my story.

Kupaki has, for the most part, remained the same tiny village in the mountains. It has undergone substantial modernization, however from the time of Panayota's affair. Today a mother is as likely to fret over her daughter being hesitant to begin dating as she is to worry about her starting too soon.

How would Thanasis and Panayota fair in today's world? Would they have acted the same way in 2005 as they had in 1935? Would their adherence to tradition have been so steadfast?

I concluded that Thanasis and Panayota were modern incarnations of their resilient and cunning ancestors. Maybe, as in the tragedies of Ancient Greece, they were figures destined to fight for their honor no matter how foolish the rest of the world may think them to be.

My sons reminded me that when Helen was taken to Troy, her loved ones did not hesitate to sacrifice their wealth and safety to rescue her. They launched a thousand ships and endured a decade of war, all to protect her honor.

EPILOGUE

"Counsel," pleased I am, but satisfied I'm not. They'll go to jail for a few years and will be among us again one day. Panayota can never be with us again. They should pay for their crime and suffer the same way my cousin did."

That is what Thanasis answered back to a defense attorney immediately after the verdict was announced in Halkida, when he was asked in court, if he was pleased with the verdict.

Socrates would, in the years to come, emigrate with his wife and children to Canada, where he would carve out a modest life for himself and his family. His return trips to Kupaki over the years continued to earn him mostly enmity from the locals, who never forgot his conviction.

And what became of George Nitsos, the man behind Panayota's murder? The year was 1967. My parents had joined us kids in Athens since 1962. During lunch one Sunday, a distant relative telephoned and told Thanasis that George had been released from prison early because he had received credit for doing jail work as the jail's church custodian.

After his release, George opened a supermarket with the help of his remaining supporters, but that enterprise failed because, as one of his partners said later, he was cheating. He then traveled to Canada and then the U. S. for various adventures before eventually returning to Greece and ultimately Kupaki. I was shocked to learn that, after insinuating himself back into village life, he was eventually accepted by most in the village.

It wasn't long before he was a regular once again at the village store, where he told jokes and acted the part of the charismatic commander once again.

In the spring of 1985, Thanasis returned to Kupaki and wanted to pay his respects to a former mailman from the nearby village Krokylion, who had served the village for many years and who had just passed away. Unable to find transportation from Kupaki to Krokylion, Thanasis, by now quite ill himself, embarked on the trip on foot, despite Polyxeni's pleas.

After a few days at the village, Father's health deteriorated further and he was forced to return to Athens for medical care. George, who was at the store when he heard the news, turned toward the church and crossed himself. "May St. George bring him back wrapped in white sheets," he said.

The remark, a reference to the tradition of bringing home the body of someone who has died away from home in white sheets, eventually found its way to Polyxeni's ears. Not normally one for confrontation and unable to find George, she asked a friend and neighbor of George to relay a message to him.

"Tell him," she said angrily, "that he was born Linatsas and will die Linatsas. Jail didn't help him change a bit. After all that has happened, he mentions Thanasis and wishes him death!"

Minutes later, George appeared at the front door of our house in the village and called Polyxeni out to talk. "Don't listen to the gossip and to what these bastards tell you here," he insisted. "It's all a lie. I didn't say anything about Thanasis."

"You talk to me like I don't know you!" Polyxeni shot back. "More than one person heard what you said."

"Thanasis shouldn't have gone on his own and on foot to Krokylion," George countered, "and I'm surprised you didn't prevent him from such a thoughtless task. That trip caused his illness."

By now Polyxeni was furious. "Thanasis put you in jail, and you dare speak his name? He is accomplished and is leaving good things behind. He has four children, eight grandchildren who care about him and protect him. What have you done? Who do you have? What are your creations? What legacy? What name? What are you going to leave behind when your day to go to St. Anthony's cemetery comes?"

In fact, George, to my knowledge, never mentioned Thanasis's name in public again. The day George was in his coffin however, on June 16, 1996, at the chapel of St. Anthony Cemetery, was an interesting one.

As soon as the priest started to give his blessing, the chapel walls began to shake. The rafters were vibrating, the ceiling lamps swaying, and the candles in the candelabras danced. A subterranean noise rumbled from beneath the chapel.

"Earthquake!" someone shouted before leading several in a mad dash for the exit.

Another jolt was felt a few minutes later at George's graveside.

AFTERWORD

IT HAS TAKEN ME YEARS to piece together this story to my
satisfaction. I didn't want filial love to blind me to the truth,
especially if the truth contradicted what I had been told by
Thanasis and others close to me.

I was fortunate to locate the court records more than fifty
years later, as the Department of Justice of Greece was holding
them over the limit of twenty-five years in order to train its
personnel using forensic errors made then.

My family, immediate and extended, reacted strongly to
my research. "It's a story that must be told," some said, "for
Panayota, if for no other reason."

Others were less supportive. "Leave the dead alone," they
said. "Let them lie peacefully in the cemetery of St Anthony."

There was one permission I felt I needed, but I could not
get: Panayota's. It was the priest of my community in Stamford,
Connecticut, who reassured me the book would be a memorial
for Panayota.

Though initially I thought everything was in the court
records or in the newspapers, I soon realized how incomplete
the official story was. I would need to interview people—dozens
and dozens of them, in Greece and America and elsewhere.
Those most likely to remember the most, because of their
age, turned out to be between eighteen and thirty years old at
the time of the murder. The youngest of my interviewees was
seventy and the oldest ninety-six. I targeted the educated more,
counting on them to elucidate the darkest areas. Big mistake.
Education had absolutely nothing to do with how well people

remembered, though it did have an impact on the kind of analysis the interviewees supplied.

I will remember fondly the wrinkled brows knitted in concentration as aging minds tried to capture elusive memories. Often, those who had supported George and Socrates couldn't recall important details. "It has been so long," they would say. "I have absolutely no memory of things." When the topic turned to events from the civil war, which preceded the murder, their memories were flawless.

One of my most revealing interviews took place in Athens in 2003 with Ntemy Mazarakis a defense attorney on both courts, by then more than eighty years old, who after several phone calls from America had finally relented and allowed me to visit her at her home. I had pored over the newspapers and the court records by then and was impressed with Ntemy' questions, each of which had invariably made an important point while at the same time sewing doubt among the jury.

November 12, 1954. George Nitsos (center) with Socrates (right), surrounded by their defense team, while the jury deliberates in Athens. The attorney with the hat is Ntemy Mazarakis. I interviewed her at her house in 2003. Second from the left with eyeglasses is the leading defense attorney.

When I arrived at her home in Kiffisia, an exclusive Athens suburb, the sun was setting in the west.

Ntemy took me to the living room of her stately stone mansion and offered me orange juice. Dressed in a plaid skirt and sporting short hair, she appeared to be quite fit for her age. I could only marvel at her poise and aged beauty.

"What can I do for you, Dr. Konandreas?" she asked.

"Lukas, please, Mrs. Mazarakis," I replied.

"Ntemy," she said, correcting me.

Without saying a word, I removed from my bag a photo that had appeared in the *Acropolis* on November 12, 1954, decision day at the trial in Athens. The photo showed the defense team surrounding Nitsos and Karaiskos. Ntemy wore a hat.

"Is this creature me?" she asked, laughing. "Where did you unearth it from, Lukas?"

For the next two hours, while a huge storm rumbled overhead, we looked at photos and traded insights.

She remembered Thanasis as soon as she noticed his bold head in a photo. "Was he your father?" she asked.

"Yes," I replied.

"Oh, were we after him! Were we targeting him! But he kept slipping away..." She paused a moment before asking suddenly, "Is he alive?"

"No. It's been over fifteen years since he died."

I asked about the defense team's strategy, especially during the second trial in Halkida, when it became clear that the accused were going to be found guilty.

"You don't realize something," she said. "We all thought—I mean all six of us on the defense team thought—that Nitsos and Karaiskos were truly innocent."

"But surely..." I was incredulous.

"I know it sounds unbelievable with the hindsight you now have, but almost up to the time the verdict of 'guilty' came, we believed in their innocence. Nitsos and Karaiskos had indeed misled us. So the strategy that you now ask about—we based it on that assumption of innocence. Near the end, we sensed it and tried to change our tactics, but the accused were not willing to even think about such a plan. Nitsos seemed to think that his money and the political power of his cousin, the journalist, and other important people were going to acquit him. He wouldn't admit the possibility of anything but a 'not guilty' plea. 'I'm completely innocent,' he used to say, 'and innocent means innocent, not innocent with diminished responsibility or any other lawyer's nonsense of that sort.' And that's what we set out to prove."

"That's unbelievable," I said, shaking my head.

"I remember," she said, combing her memory, "that night near the end of the trial when that woman, Nitsos's cousin, was on the witness stand. She told the court that Panayota was always dressed by her husband in silk and that was the only way she would go out. At that point, the judge, who was extremely sharp, ordered the court clerks to open the box that contained the blood-spattered dress Panayota wore the night she was murdered. It was a robe, a cotton house robe. It didn't make sense that Panayota had changed into a robe if she had indeed planned to return later to the dinner party. I was the only defense attorney in the court that night, and it was very late. I saw the reaction of the jury, and I knew we were losing—and losing badly. It was almost midnight. When I got back from the court, I was confused and agitated, and I must have sounded so frantic that the other attorneys showed up immediately at the my hotel, when I phoned them to have a meeting."

"Why did you do that?" I asked.

"I wanted to explore a different scenario, one I had pondered before the trial in Athens, and see if we could present it, even at that late stage of the trial, as a true account of incidents."

"What was that scenario?" I asked eagerly.

"I wanted from the beginning to say that Nitsos was alone down at the Zakkas house and Panayota had stayed home. Then someone had taken her by force from their home and killed her by the ravine, and no one knew about it until Nitsos decided to leave the Zakkas home and walk toward his house and found her dead in the middle of the path."

I cocked my head in disbelief.

"Well, I know it didn't make sense," she said, reading the expression on my face, "but that tells you how misled, tired, agitated, desperate, almost out of reality I was by then, along with some of the other attorneys."

I thought of asking about the leading defense attorney, whose closing remarks either intentionally or subconsciously had bordered on deranged. But I chose to keep quiet.

Ntemy then pieced together several other inappropriate things George had done during the trial, and when I told her how he had behaved after being released from jail, she appeared shocked.

"Nitsos broke more commandments than Moses wrote," she said, to my amusement.

Perhaps depressed by the memory of everything he had done, she decided to change the topic.

"So tell me about yourself. I don't remember much about Thanasis Konandreas's family."

"Well, I have a sister and two brothers," I replied. "They all have good families."

Ntemy then asked me about the professions my siblings pursued and I told her.

"It's good that your father could afford all that," an impressed Ntemy said. "He was well off, as I remember."

I had to smile at that. "Well off he was not," I said, correcting her. "In fact, the prosecution attorneys almost did charitable work for Thanasis, and our family was left penniless after Halkida."

Then I told her about the free governmental policy that helped our education in the early '60's. "We were lucky, very fortunate," I concluded.

"No, no," Ntemy interrupted. "Your father possessed the fortitude and the honor to pursue justice against all odds.

It seems that God has rewarded his good deeds through his children."

I thanked Ntemy and exited her house walking into the pelting rain her words of praise for my father resonating in my ears. As I drove back home to another suburb of the big city, my mind wondered through the names of people, besides my immediate family, who should also receive praise and thanks for their role in this story. I recognized many, but I placed at the top of my list the juror in the Athens trial, who after seven hours of jury arguments and likely pressures for the final verdict, did not hesitate to disagree with the other nine jurors who voted "Innocent." His dissenting vote opened the door for the second trial. On behalf of my aunt and father, thank you Demosthenes Dapontes.

INDEX OF NAMES
(DRAMATIS PERSONAE)

BELOW IS A LIST OF names used in this book. Each name is followed by a short description of the person or location in question. Any person's name that differs from his or her real name is followed by the real name in parenthesis. Some names have been changed, mostly for the reader's benefit.

Aggelo (Aggeliki Kufasimis): Prosecution witness at Halkida. Sister of Thanasis Konandreas.

Alekos Tsipras (Alexandros Tsipras): Professor of literature. Cousin of Polyxeni Konandreas.

Alex Nitsos (Alexandros Nitsos): Brother of George Nitsos.

Aliki (Aggeliki Gumas): Mother of Polyxeni Konandreas.

Basil (Vasilios Kolimbaris): Attorney. Prosecution witness on the second trial.

Dapontes, Demosthenes: Juror at the trial in Athens. Likely the only juror to dissent.

Effie (Efthemia Tsatuhas): Prosecution witness at the Halkida trial only.

George Nitsos (Georgios Nitsos): Husband of Panayota. Also known by the nickname Linatsas.

Georgia: Wife of Dr. Lukas Konandreas, M.D., and a doctor herself.

Halkida: The city where the second trial took place.

James (Demetrios Soulias): Brother of Panayota

Katina: Girlfriend of George Nitsos. Defense witness.

Krokylion: The bigger village next to Kupaki.

Kupaki: The village where the murder takes place.

Marula (Marula Mitsakis): The village woman who told Panayota about George Nitsos and Katina.

Mary (Maria Brumas): Wife of Takis. Prosecution witness.

Mia (Efthemia Konandreas): Mother of Thanasis Konandreas.

Mitros (Demetrios Konandreas): Uncle of Thanasis. Lived next door to Thanasis in Kupaki.

Ntemy Mazarakis (Despina Mazarakis): Defense attorney. Interviewed by author decades after trial.

Ntinos (Konstantinos Papaioannou): Village man and self-appointed jester. Prosecution witness.

Papadia (Vasiliki Papakonstantinou): Sister of Thanasis and wife of Papazois.

Papazois (Zois Papakonstantinou): The village priest. Prosecution witness and Thanasis's brother-in-law.

Poly (Polyxeni Saitis): The young beauty who George Nitsos courted in the mid '40s.

Skevi (Paraskevi Soulias): Mother of Panayota.

Socrates (Sokratis Karaiskos): George Nitsos's best man and close friend who stood trial along with him.

Takis (Panagiotis Brumas): Prosecution witness. Shepherd in partnership with George Nitsos and Thanasis Konandreas.

Thanasis (Thanasis Konandreas): Cousin of Panayota. Husband of Polyxeni. Father of Lukas Konandreas.

Tsipanos (Panos Tsipras): Professor of Theology. Cousin of Polyxeni Konandreas.

Vas (Vasilios Kalantzis): The man with whom George Nitsos had an ongoing feud. Prosecution witness.

Lukas Konandreas 2013 and circa 1954

Lukas Konandreas M.D. one of four children, was born at Kupaki, a small mountain village in central Greece.

He finished elementary school there and high school in Athens, Greece.

After graduating from the Medical School of the University of Athens, he immigrated to Toronto, Canada, and from there he did medical training in Chicago and Fresno, California. He practiced Emergency Medicine in Sacramento California for about six years and from there he moved to Connecticut, where he organized an Urgent Care Center, which he still directs after 30 years.

He is married to Georgia, a Doctor of Psychology, and has two sons.

Book cover: On the right is Thanasis Konandreas at the witness stand

ACKNOWLEDGMENTS

THANKS ARE DUE FIRST AND foremost to my wife, Georgia, who did not only urge me to write this chronicle, but supported me throughout, making sure no part of the truth was ever or in any way compromised.

My appreciation to my sons Johnathan and Peter, who gave me many ideas on difficult issues and helped immensely on my computer related problems.

My gratitude to author William Greenleaf, of Greenleaf Literary Services, for his help and patience in writing this book.

Thanks to Mahesh Nair for his help as creative consultant.

Finally, my gratitude to folks at Streetlight Graphics for their work on the cover and interior and providing helpful advice throughout the publishing process.

Lukas Konandreas, M.D.

**DEDICATED TO MY PARENTS
THANASIS AND POLYXENI.**

CPSIA information can be obtained
at www.ICGtesting.com
Printed in the USA
BVHW031022241218
536347BV00004B/405/P